Rescued

CRITICAL READING SERIES

Rescued

21 Stories of Daring Rescues—with Exercises for Developing Reading Comprehension and Critical Thinking Skills

Henry Billings

Melissa Billings

JAMESTOWN PUBLISHERS

a division of NTC/CONTEMPORARY PUBLISHING GROUP
Lincolnwood, Illinois USA

ISBN 0-89061-323-0

Published by Jamestown Publishers,
a division of NTC/Contemporary Publishing Group, Inc.
4255 West Touhy Avenue
Lincolnwood (Chicago), Illinois 60712-1975, U.S.A.
©1999 NTC/Contemporary Publishing Group, Inc.

7 8 9 10 11 12 13 14 1 13 09 08 07 06 05 04

CONTENTS

UNIT THREE

To the Student

Most of the time, we are bombarded by bad news. Every day, we hear about wars, crimes, and violence. We may begin to think that the world is a pretty scary, dangerous, and cruel place. However the stories in this book offer proof that the world has a kinder, more generous side, too. In fact, they prove that, especially in emergencies, we humans have an amazing ability to forget about our own needs while we try to save someone else's life.

Each lesson in this book tells the story of an exciting rescue. The details about each event were found in newspaper articles and magazines. The heroes of these rescues are normal, everyday people just like you. Most of them don't consider themselves to be heroes. When they talk about their rescues, they may say that all they did was see a need and respond in the only logical way. But what else is a hero than someone who forgets himself or herself just to help another? As you read each article, think about what you might have done in the same situation. Could you be a hero, too?

Rescued is for students who already read fairly well but who want to read faster and to increase their understanding of what they read. If you complete the 21 lessons—reading the articles and completing the exercises—you will surely increase your reading speed and improve your reading comprehension and critical thinking skills. Also, because these exercises include items of the types often found on state and national tests, learning how to complete them will prepare you for tests you may have to take in the future.

How to Use This Book

About the Book. *Rescued* contains three units, each of which includes seven lessons. Each lesson begins with an article about an unusual event, person, or group. The article is followed by a group of four reading comprehension exercises and a set of three critical thinking exercises. The reading comprehension exercises will help you understand the article. The critical thinking exercises will help you think about what you have read and how it relates to your own experience.

At the end of each lesson, you will also have the opportunity to give your personal response to some aspect of the article and then to assess how well you understood what you read.

The Sample Lesson. Working through the sample lesson, the first lesson in the book, with your class or group will demonstrate how a lesson is organized. The sample lesson explains how to complete the exercises and score your answers. The correct answers for the sample exercises and sample scores are printed in lighter type. In some cases, explanations of the correct answers are given. The explanations will help you understand how to think through these question types.

If you have any questions about how to complete the exercises or score them, this is the time to get the answers.

Working Through Each Lesson. Begin each lesson by looking at the photographs and reading the captions. Before you read, predict what you think the article will be about. Then read the article.

Sometimes your teacher may decide to time your reading. Timing helps you keep track of and increase your reading speed. If you have been timed, enter your reading time in the box at the end of the lesson. Then use the Words-per-Minute Table to find your reading speed, and record your speed on the Reading Speed graph at the end of the unit.

Next complete the Reading Comprehension and Critical Thinking exercises. The directions for each exercise will tell you how to mark your answers. When you have finished all four Reading Comprehension exercises, use the answer key provided by your teacher to check your work. Follow the directions after each exercise to find your score. Record your Reading Comprehension scores on the graph at the end of each unit. Then check your answers to the Author's Approach, Summarizing and Paraphrasing, and Critical Thinking exercises. Fill in the Critical Thinking chart at the end of each unit with your evaluation of your work and comments about your progress.

At the end of each unit you will also complete a Compare/Contrast chart. The completed chart will help you see what the articles have in common, and it will give you an opportunity to examine what you think and feel about each of these rescues and the people who became involved in them.

SAMPLE LESSON

IN THE NICK OF TIME

Anthony Falzo with the two children he rescued, Todd and Scott Pritchard

As Katie Pritchard unloaded bags of groceries from the trunk of her car on May 1, 1989, her sons Todd and Scott played happily in the driveway. The family lived at the end of a dead-end street in Ramsey, New Jersey. So Katie was not worried about her kids wandering out to the street and getting hit by a car. But she often warned three-year-old Todd not to go near the railroad tracks. The tracks were less than 300 feet from the house, just beyond a cluster of trees.

2   After putting away her first load of groceries, Katie returned to her car to get more bags. She saw the boys still at play. Katie also heard the roar of a passenger express train as it rolled by. Then she went back into the house with another load of grocery bags.

3   Despite their mother's warnings, Todd and his 18-month-old brother were attracted by the sound of the speeding train. They walked through the trees and knelt down on the tracks. What the little boys didn't know was that a second train was heading straight for them.

4   Just over a slight rise to the west, a 19-car freight train slowly made its way up

the incline. Rich Campana, the engineer, saw the overhead lights give the "all-clear." The passenger express train was far down the tracks. So Campana pulled the throttle to resume full speed. Standing next to him in the cab was conductor Anthony Falzo. Falzo, a 17-year veteran of the railroad, was sharing some small talk with Campana. But as the train reached the top of the rise, the two men noticed something on the tracks about 800 yards ahead. What was it? It appeared to be two bundles or boxes—one yellow and one red. "Then the yellow one moved," said Falzo, "and we realized it was two kids."

5 Campana slammed on the train's brake and blasted his air horn. Falzo knew right away that the train was going too fast to stop in time. Immediately he rushed out the engine's cab door and out onto its narrow running board. He quickly made his way to the front of the engine, then climbed down a steel ladder to the last rung. There he hung, at the front of the train, about two feet above the roadbed. Frantically he waved and shouted at the kids, telling them to get off the tracks. They didn't move. Falzo later said that they just looked up "as if we could steer around them."

6 Meanwhile Katie heard the air horn and the screech of the train's brakes. Her heart pounded as she raced outside. Just one look around told her the truth. Todd and Scott were gone! She knew that they must be on the tracks.

7 Falzo thought about jumping off the train and trying to run ahead of it to save the little boys. But even as the train slowed down, Falzo knew he couldn't outrun it. So this 35-year-old former gymnast formed another plan. He decided to leap off the train just as it neared the children. That way he might be able to scoop up the boys and get them off the track in time. Falzo would have to time his jump exactly. If he leaped too soon, the train would beat him to the kids. If he jumped too late, the train would crush the boys beneath its wheels.

8 Luckily, Falzo had a very good sense of timing. At the last possible instant, he leaped from the train. He took two giant strides and grabbed the children. With one child tucked under each arm, he pressed Todd and Scott down into the roadbed gravel. The outer edge of the train passed just inches over their heads.

9 Falzo wasn't quite fast enough to pull both children and himself completely out of the way. The black steel blade on the front of the engine ripped open the back of his quilted work vest. The blade also clipped Scott under the chin. The blow opened a wound which drenched the toddler's face in blood. The force "[snapped] his head back like a rag doll,"

Todd and Scott Pritchard were playing in the roadbed of the railroad tracks when Anthony Falzo leapt from the train to pull them out of the way.

remembered Falzo. "I thought his neck was broken."

10   When the train finally stopped, the third car was perched just a couple of inches over their heads. But the boys were safe. Luckily, Scott's cut wasn't serious. After 13 stitches, he was as good as new. "There's no word in *Webster's*," said Katie Pritchard, "that can express our deepest, everlasting appreciation to Tony [Falzo] for what he did."

11   Reporters later asked Anthony Falzo, who had no children of his own, if he hesitated at all before risking his life to rescue Todd and Scott. "No," he answered. "All I could think was that those two little kids have their whole lives still ahead of them, and if I do nothing, they're dead.

There was no way I could let that happen."

If you have been timed while reading this article, enter your reading time below. Then turn to the Words-per-Minute Table on page 71 and look up your reading speed (words per minute). Enter your reading speed on the graph on page 72.

Reading Time: Sample Lesson

3 : 01

Minutes   Seconds

A | Finding the Main Idea

One statement below expresses the main idea of the article. One statement is too general, or too broad. The other statement explains only part of the article; it is too narrow. Label the statements using the following key:

M—Main Idea   **B—Too Broad**   **N—Too Narrow**

___B___   1. Little children often fail to understand the danger they put themselves in. [This statement is true, but it is *too broad*. This article is about a particular danger—a speeding train— as well as an exciting rescue.]

___M___   2. After spotting two little boys sitting on railroad tracks in the path of his speeding train, conductor Anthony Falzo leaped from the train and scooped them to safety . [This statement is the *main idea*. It tells you what danger threatened the little boys and describes their rescue.]

___N___   3. Katie Pritchard and her two sons Todd and Scott lived less than 300 yards from railroad tracks. [This statement is true, but it is *too narrow*. It presents only one fact from the article.]

___15___   Score 15 points for a correct M answer.

___10___   Score 5 points for each correct B or N answer.

___25___   **Total Score:** Finding the Main Idea

B | Recalling Facts

How well do you remember the facts in the article? Put an X in the box next to the answer that correctly completes each statement about the article.

1. The Pritchard family lived in
☐ a. Texas.
☐ b. Illinois.
☒ c. New Jersey.

2. When the engineer of the freight train saw the "all-clear" lights, he
☐ a. slammed on the brakes.
☒ b. went back to full speed.
☐ c. blasted his air horn.

3. Falzo rejected the idea of jumping off the train and running ahead to save the boys because he
☐ a. was too frightened to try it.
☐ b. was too old.
☒ c. knew he couldn't outrun the train.

4. After Falzo grabbed the boys, he
☒ a. pressed them down into the roadbed gravel.
☐ b. threw them clear of the tracks.
☐ c. hopped back on the train with them in his arms.

5. The only person who was injured in the rescue was
☐ a. Todd.
☒ b. Scott.
☐ c. Anthony Falzo.

Score 5 points for each correct answer.

___25___   **Total Score:** Recalling Facts

C | Making Inferences

When you combine your own experience and information from a text to draw a conclusion that is not directly stated in that text, you are making an inference. Below are five statements that may or may not be inferences based on information in the article. Label the statements using the following key:

C—Correct Inference   **F—Faulty Inference**

_____F_____ 1. Katie Pritchard was not aware of the danger to her boys that the railroad tracks presented. [This is a *faulty* inference. The article mentions that Katie had often warned the children not to go near the railroad tracks.]

_____C_____ 2. The engineer and the conductor of the train did not expect to see the little boys on the tracks. [This is a *correct* inference. The article says that the engineer had been given the "all-clear" signal, indicating that the tracks ahead were clear.]

_____C_____ 3. A speeding train cannot stop quickly. [This is a *correct* inference. The article says that even though the engineer applied the train's brakes, he didn't expect to be able to stop the train in time to save the children.]

_____C_____ 4. The fact that Falzo had been a gymnast probably helped him rescue the children. [This is a *correct* inference. Through gymnastics, Falzo developed the flexibility, timing, and body control to successfully jump off a speeding train and grab the boys.]

_____F_____ 5. All 19 cars of the freight train passed over Falzo and the boys before the train could stop. [This is a *faulty* inference. The article states that the train stopped with only the third car just a few inches over the heads of the boys.]

> Score 5 points for each correct answer.
>
> _____25_____ **Total Score:** Making Inferences

D | Using Words Precisely

Each numbered sentence below contains an underlined word or phrase from the article. Following the sentence are three definitions. One definition is closest to the meaning of the underlined word. One definition is opposite or nearly opposite. Label those two definitions using the following key. Do not label the remaining definition.

C—Closest   **O—Opposite or Nearly Opposite**

1. Just over a slight rise to the west, a 19-car freight train slowly made its way up the <u>incline</u>.

   _____O_____ a. downward slope

   _____ b. curve in the road

   _____C_____ c. gradual rise

2. So Campana pulled the throttle to <u>resume</u> full speed.

   _____ a. enjoy

   _____O_____ b. stop

   _____C_____ c. begin again

3. <u>Frantically</u> he waved and shouted at the kids, telling them to get off the tracks.

   _____C_____ a. in a highly excited way

   _____O_____ b. in a calm way

   _____ c. in a silly way

4. "There's no word in *Webster's*," said Katie Pritchard, "that can express our deepest, everlasting <u>appreciation</u> to Tony [Falzo] for what he did."

   _____ a. curiosity

   _____O_____ b. resentment

   _____C_____ c. gratitude

5. Reporters later asked Anthony Falzo...if he <u>hesitated</u> at all before risking his life to rescue Todd and Scott.

_____C_____ a. held back because of doubt

_____ b. shivered

_____O_____ c. acted quickly and certainly

_____15_____	Score 3 points for each correct C answer.
_____10_____	Score 2 points for each correct O answer.
_____25_____	**Total Score:** Using Words Precisely

Enter the four total scores in the spaces below, and add them together to find your Reading Comprehension Score. Then record your score on the graph on page 73.

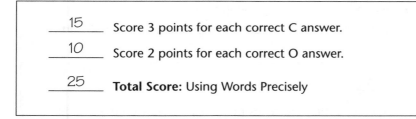

Score	Question Type	Sample Lesson
_____25_____	Finding the Main Idea	
_____25_____	Recalling Facts	
_____25_____	Making Inferences	
_____25_____	Using Words Precisely	
_____100_____	**Reading Comprehension Score**	

Author's Approach

Put an X in the box next to the correct answer.

1. What does the author mean by the statement "Falzo, a 17-year veteran of the railroad, was sharing some small talk with Campana"?

☐ a. Falzo and Campana tried to talk as little as possible since they were not friends.

☒ b. Falzo and Campana were talking about nothing special.

☐ c. Falzo and Campana's conversations were always boring.

2. The main purpose of the first paragraph is to

☒ a. introduce the setting of the article.

☐ b. describe Katie Pritchard's personality.

☐ c. compare Katie Pritchard's two sons.

3. From the statements below, choose those that you believe the author would agree with.

☒ a. Little children who live near dangers such as railroad tracks should be supervised constantly.

☐ b. No one should live near railroad tracks.

☐ c. The railroads are to blame if anyone gets killed by trains.

4. What does the author imply by saying "Falzo later said that they [the boys] just looked up "as if we could steer around them"?

☐ a. The boys understood that they were in danger but were paralyzed by their terror.

☐ b. The boys thought that the danger was fun.

☒ c. The boys didn't think they were in any danger.

_____4_____ Number of correct answers
Record your personal assessment of your work on the Critical Thinking Chart on page 74.

Summarizing and Paraphrasing

Put an X in the box next to the correct answer.

1. Below are summaries of the article. Choose the summary that says all the most important things about the article but in the fewest words.

☐ a. In a very exciting rescue, two little boys were saved, thanks to the fast work of Anthony Falzo. [This summary leaves out almost all of the important details, such as the kind of danger the boys faced, who Anthony Falzo was, and what he did to save them.]

☐ b. Katie Pritchard was putting away her groceries when her two boys three-year-old Todd and 18-month-old Scott were attracted by the sound of a nearby train. After the train went by, they knelt on the tracks. Very soon, a freight train sped toward them, but they didn't move. Conductor Anthony Falzo decided that since the train would not be able to stop, he would have to run ahead of the train, scoop up the children, and hold them close to the ground while the train passed over them. That is what he did, and he rescued the children from certain death. [This summary presents most of the important ideas from the article but includes too many unnecessary details.]

☒ c. Two little boys left their mother and knelt on nearby railroad tracks, directly in the path of a speeding train. Conductor Anthony Falzo saved their lives by leaping off the train at the last instant before impact and holding the children close to the ground while the train passed over them. Falzo earned the boys' mother's eternal gratitude. [This summary says all the most important things about the article in the fewest words.]

2. Read the statement about the article below. Then read the paraphrase of that statement. Choose the reason that best tells why the paraphrase does not say the same thing as the statement.

Statement: At first, the engineer and conductor could not make out what was on the tracks 800 yards ahead of them.

Paraphrase: Although at first the engineer and conductor didn't know what was on the tracks about 800 yards ahead of them, when the yellow shape moved, they realized that the shapes were actually two children.

☒ a. Paraphrase says too much. [The first statement simply says that the conductor could not identify what was on the tracks. The second statement adds more information—that they were able to identify the objects when one child moved.]

☐ b. Paraphrase doesn't say enough.

☐ c. Paraphrase doesn't agree with the statement about the article.

___2___ Number of correct answers

Record your personal assessment of your work on the Critical Thinking Chart on page 74.

Critical Thinking

Follow the directions provided for questions 1 and 3. Put an X in the box next to the correct answer for the other questions.

1. For each statement below, write O if it expresses an opinion or write F if it expresses a fact.

___F___ a. Scott Pritchard needed 13 stitches to close his wound.

___F___ b. The Pritchards lived less than 300 yards from the railroad tracks.

___O___ c. Anthony Falzo seems like a nice person who likes children.

2. From what Anthony Falzo said, you can predict that if he were presented with the same situation again, he would

☒ a. make the same decision and try the rescue again.

☐ b. be too afraid to try such a risky stunt.

☐ c. ask someone else to rescue the children.

3. Choose from the letters below to correctly complete the following statement. Write the letters on the lines.

On the positive side, ___*b*___, but on the negative side ___*a*___

a. everyone, including Falzo and Katie Pritchard, was thoroughly frightened

b. the children lived through the experience

c. Anthony Falzo tried to wave the boys off the tracks

4. What was the cause of the cut under Scott's chin?

☐ a. His chin scraped against the gravel in the roadbed.

☒ b. The blade on the front of the engine hit him there.

☐ c. He fell onto the track just as Falzo grabbed him.

5. What did you have to do to answer question 3?

☐ a. find a cause (why something happened)

☐ b. find an opinion (what someone thinks about something)

☒ c. find a contrast (how things are different)

___5___ Number of correct answers

Record your personal assessment of your work on the Critical Thinking Chart on page 74.

Personal Response

A question I would like answered by Anthony Falzo is

[Write any qustion you would ask Anthony Falzo if you could

meet him face-to-face.]

_____

_____

Self-Assessment

I'm proud of how I answered question # _____ in section _____ because

[Choose one question that you feel you answered well. Explain

why you liked your answer.]

_____

_____

_____

CRITICAL THINKING

Self-Assessment

To get the most out of the Critical Reading series program, you need to take charge of your own progress in improving your reading comprehension and critical thinking skills. Here are some of the features that help you work on those essential skills.

Reading Comprehension Exercises. Complete these exercises immediately after reading the article. They help you recall what you have read, understand the stated and implied main ideas, and add words to your working vocabulary.

Critical Thinking Skills Exercises. These exercises help you focus on the author's approach and purpose, recognize and generate summaries and paraphrases, and identify relationships between ideas.

Personal Response and Self-assessment. Questions in this category help you relate the articles to your personal experience and give you the opportunity to evaluate your understanding of the information in that lesson.

Compare and Contrast Charts. At the end of each unit you will complete a Compare and Contrast chart. The completed chart helps you see what the articles have in common and gives you an opportunity to explore your own ideas about the topics discussed in the articles.

The Graphs. The graphs and charts at the end of each unit enable you to keep track of your progress. Check your graphs regularly with your teacher. Decide whether your progress is satisfactory or whether you need additional work on some skills. What types of exercises are you having difficulty with? Talk with your teacher about ways to work on the skills in which you need the most practice.

UNIT ONE

SAVING J.J. THE WHALE

Having grown too big for the San Diego Zoo, J.J. is loaded onto a truck and transported to the ocean, where she will be released to live in her natural habitat.

The little baby whale was lost. Just three days old, she still had her umbilical cord attached. Fortunately, some workers spotted her around 8 A.M. on January 10, 1997. She was floundering around about a quarter of a mile from Venice Pier in Marina del Rey, California. The baby's mother was nowhere in sight. The grey whale was far too young to survive on her own. She either needed to find her mother so she could nurse, or she had to be saved by human beings so she could be fed by bottle.

2 California grey whales are a protected species. By federal law, they are supposed to be left alone unless they are beached. But this little whale clearly needed a helping hand. So a group of lifeguards tried to calm the baby whale and get her to swim back out to sea. That way, they hoped, her mother might find her. Or maybe the baby whale could then hook up with other migrating grey whales headed south for the winter.

3 At first it looked as if the lifeguards' efforts would work. The whale beached

herself three times but then finally made it beyond the breaking surf. That night she disappeared beneath the surface. Perhaps, thought the lifeguards, she would be all right after all.

4   The next morning, however, brought a sad sight. The 13-foot, 8-inch baby whale hadn't found her mother. She hadn't met a migrating pod of grey whales, either. Instead, she could be seen swimming around in circles just a quarter of a mile from the shore. She seemed confused and listless. "[Her] chance of survival in the wild [was] slim or zero at [that] point," said John Heyning, an expert on mammals.

5   For the baby whale, soon nicknamed J.J., it was now a matter of life or death. (She was named after the late Judi Jones, a leader in the move to rescue sea mammals in distress.) Rescue workers got permission from the government to attempt a shallow water rescue. They jumped into the water and began splashing water to coax the whale toward the shore. At first, J.J. didn't move. At last, she got the hint and slowly moved toward the beach on her own. A large flatbed truck was waiting at the water's edge. The bed had been tipped down toward sand. The plan was to slip a giant sling under the 1,670-pound whale and then slide her onto the truck.

6   The rescue team got the sling under J.J. But they still could not move the heavy whale. "We need help," shouted one of the rescuers to the crowd which had gathered to watch the rescue. Along the shore, Los Angeles police officers had been holding back onlookers and reporters. In a flash, 11 of these officers plunged into the

sea. "When we were trying to stabilize the whale these officers jumped right into the water without hesitation with all their clothes on," said Peter Wallerstein, one of the rescuers. "If it wasn't for [them], that whale would have died." Other volunteers pitched in as well. Two U.S. attorneys riding their bikes along the beach helped

Grey whales breed off the Baja Peninsula in Mexico and Southwestern California. The lifespan of a grey whale is 60 to 80 years.

out. So, too, did a man who had come to the beach to scatter his father's cremated ashes in the Pacific.

7 Together the group slipped the sling under J.J. and hooked it to a line on the truck. Then they slowly cranked the whale up and onto the truck. At the same time, some of the rescuers dumped pail after pail of seawater over the bewildered mammal. It took nearly 20 minutes for them to settle J.J. securely on the flatbed. When they did, spectators cheered and whistled in approval.

8 J.J. was covered with wet towels to keep her cool and moist. She was then driven 120 miles down the highway to Sea World in San Diego. In spite of those efforts, her chances of survival were still slim at best. She arrived at Sea World comatose and nearly starved to death.

9 Doctors gave her emergency aid and as much food as she could handle. In the beginning, she dined on baby formula mixed with crushed herring and vitamins. Within just a few days, J.J. began to perk up. Soon she was gaining as much as two pounds an hour! Before long, she became a major Sea World celebrity. The park began to sell all sorts of J.J. souvenirs. There were also J.J. banners lining the entrance to Sea World.

10 There was no way, however, that J.J. could stay at Sea World. After 15 months she had grown too big. The 1,670-pound weakling had turned into a 31-foot, 19,200-pound behemoth. (A fully-grown adult female grey whale can be as long as 55 feet and weigh as much as 74,000 pounds.) She became the largest mammal ever kept in captivity. And, in any event, most people felt that J.J. belonged back in the sea. So, on March 31, 1998, the whale was once again loaded onto a truck. She then took an 11-mile trip to the ocean where she was transferred to the U.S. Coast Guard cutter *Conifer*. About two miles off the coast of Point Loma, J.J. was lowered over the side. Then chief boatswain mate Thomas Young gave a command not often heard aboard a ship at sea: "Release the whale!"

11 At first, J.J. started swimming back to San Diego—the only home she knew. But before anyone on the *Conifer* could get too nervous, her instincts took over and she made an abrupt U-turn. She headed further out to sea—fast. "J.J. did what a wild animal will do," said Tom Reidarson, a veterinarian at Sea World. "She got the heck away from human beings as fast as she could. It's not that she doesn't like us. It's just that she doesn't need us anymore." 🍃

If you have been timed while reading this article, enter your reading time below. Then turn to the Words-per-Minute Table on page 71 and look up your reading speed (words per minute). Enter your reading speed on the graph on page 72.

Reading Time: Lesson 1

3 : 28
Minutes   Seconds

A | Finding the Main Idea

One statement below expresses the main idea of the article. One statement is too general, or too broad. The other statement explains only part of the article; it is too narrow. Label the statements using the following key:

M—Main Idea   **B—Too Broad**   **N—Too Narrow**

___N___ 1. When rescuers had trouble moving a baby whale, police officers waded into the water to help.

___M___ 2. Animal lovers helped a young whale they called J.J. to survive without its mother and to find its way back to its home in the ocean.

___B___ 3. Sometimes animals need the help of humans to survive.

___15___ Score 15 points for a correct M answer.

___10___ Score 5 points for each correct B or N answer.

___25___ **Total Score:** Finding the Main Idea

B | Recalling Facts

How well do you remember the facts in the article? Put an X in the box next to the answer that correctly completes each statement about the article.

1. At first, lifeguards hoped to get the baby whale to swim further out to sea so she could
☐ a. die farther away from the beach.
☒ b. meet and join a group of migrating whales.
☐ c. swim into a sling for transporting to Sea World.

2. The baby whale was nicknamed J.J. in honor of a
☐ a. lifeguard who died while trying to rescue her.
☐ b. U.S. president.
☒ c. woman who worked to rescue sea mammals.

3. J.J. was driven to Sea World in
☐ a. Orlando, Florida.
☐ b. Cleveland, Ohio.
☒ c. San Diego, California.

4. At Sea World, J.J. was fed
☒ a. crushed herring and vitamins.
☐ b. plankton.
☐ c. a strict vegetable diet.

✗ 5. J.J. was released into the ocean from a
☒ a. large flat-bed truck.
☐ b. U.S. Coast Guard cutter.
☐ c. helicopter.

Score 5 points for each correct answer.

___20___ **Total Score:** Recalling Facts

C | Making Inferences

When you combine your own experience and information from a text to draw a conclusion that is not directly stated in that text, you are making an inference. Below are five statements that may or may not be inferences based on information in the article. Label the statements using the following key:

C—Correct Inference   **F—Faulty Inference**

_C_ ~~F~~ 1. Usually, wild animals have a better chance of surviving if humans don't interfere with them.

_C_ 2. Sea mammal rescuers have great respect for Judi Jones.

_F_ 3. Whale rescue is a common, everyday occurrence on California beaches.

_C_ 4. If it weren't for the help from humans, J.J. probably wouldn't have survived.

_F_ 5. Sea World is making plans to capture an even bigger whale than J.J.

Score 5 points for each correct answer.

_20_ **Total Score:** Making Inferences

D | Using Words Precisely

Each numbered sentence below contains an underlined word or phrase from the article. Following the sentence are three definitions. One definition is closest to the meaning of the underlined word. One definition is opposite or nearly opposite. Label those two definitions using the following key. Do not label the remaining definition.

C—Closest   **O—Opposite or Nearly Opposite**

1. She [the whale] seemed confused and <u>listless</u>.

_C_ a. without energy or spirit

_C_ b. lost

_O_ c. lively

2. They jumped into the water and began splashing water to <u>coax</u> the whale <u>toward</u> the shore.

_O_ a. turn...away from

___ b. see...from

_C_ c. attract...in the direction of

3. "When we were trying to <u>stabilize</u> the whale these officers jumped right into the water..."said Peter Wallerstein, one of the rescuers.

_O_ a. make shaky

_C_ b. make steady

✗ _O_ c. frighten

4. She arrived at Sea World <u>comatose</u> and nearly starved to death.

✗ _C_ a. tired

_C_ b. unconscious

_O_ c. alert

5. The 1,670-pound weakling had turned into a 31-foot, 19,200-pound underline{behemoth}.

_____O_____ a. small and weak animal

_____C_____ b. huge and mighty animal

_____ c. clever animal

_____12_____ Score 3 points for each correct C answer.

_____8_____ Score 2 points for each correct O answer.

_____20_____ **Total Score:** Using Words Precisely

Enter the four total scores in the spaces below, and add them together to find your Reading Comprehension Score. Then record your score on the graph on page 73.

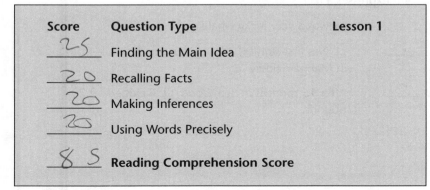

Score	Question Type	Lesson 1
25	Finding the Main Idea	
20	Recalling Facts	
20	Making Inferences	
20	Using Words Precisely	
85	**Reading Comprehension Score**	

Author's Approach

Put an X in the box next to the correct answer.

1. The main purpose of the first paragraph is to
   - ☐ a. set a sorrowful mood.
   - ☒ b. explain the problem to the reader.
   - ☐ c. compare baby whales with mature whales.

2. Which of the following statements from the article best describes J.J. before her rescue?
   - ☒ a. "The little baby whale was lost."
   - ☐ b. "Within just a few days, J.J. began to perk up."
   - ☐ c. "She headed further out to sea—fast. "

3. From the statements below, choose those that you believe the author would agree with.
   - ☐ a. People should never interfere with the lives of wild animals.
   - ✗ ☐ b. Rescuers really wanted J.J. to survive.
   - ☒ c. Many people are eager to help animals in trouble.

4. How is the author's purpose for writing the article expressed in paragraph 11?
   - ☐ a. In this paragraph, the author points out that San Diego was the only home that J.J. knew.
   - ✗ ☐ b. In this paragraph, a veterinarian explains that wild animals belong far away from humans.
   - ☒ c. In this paragraph, the author points out that J.J. at first started to swim back to San Diego.

   _____2.5_____ Number of correct answers

   Record your personal assessment of your work on the Critical Thinking Chart on page 74.

CRITICAL THINKING

Summarizing and Paraphrasing

Follow the directions provided for questions 1 and 2. Put an X in the box next to the correct answer for question 3.

1. Look for the important ideas and events in paragraphs 3 and 4. Summarize those paragraphs in one or two sentences.

   They were talking about the
   lost whale

2. Complete the following one-sentence summary of the article using the lettered phrases from the phrase bank below. Write the letters on the lines.

> **Phrase Bank:**
> a. efforts to save the whale
> b. the release of J.J.
> c. the sighting of a lost baby whale near Marina del Rey

The article about J.J. the whale begins with __c__, goes on to explain __a__, and ends with __b__.

3. Read the statement about the article below. Then read the paraphrase of that statement. Choose the reason that best tells why the paraphrase does not say the same thing as the statement.

Statement: Rescuers slipped a sling under J.J., hooked it to a line on a truck, and cranked the whale up onto the truck.

Paraphrase: Carefully, rescuers pulled J.J. up onto a truck.

- ☐ a. Paraphrase says too much.
- ☒ b. Paraphrase doesn't say enough.
- ☐ c. Paraphrase doesn't agree with the statement about the article.

> _3_ Number of correct answers
>
> Record your personal assessment of your work on the Critical Thinking Chart on page 74.

Critical Thinking

Follow the directions provided for questions 1 and 4. Put an X in the box next to the correct answer for the other questions.

1. For each statement below, write O if it expresses an opinion or write F if it expresses a fact.

   __O__ a. J.J. was a very lucky whale.

   __F__ b. J.J. was first sighted about a quarter of a mile from a pier in Marina del Rey.

   __F__ c. After 15 months at Sea World, J.J. weighed 19,200 pounds.

2. From the article, you can predict that if J.J. had died,

☐ a. no one would have cared much.

☒ b. the rescuers would have been unhappy.

☐ c. veterinarians would have been very surprised.

3. What was the effect of the treatment that J.J. received at Sea World?

☐ a. She became bewildered.

☐ b. She became weaker and weaker.

☒ c. She survived and grew.

4. Which paragraphs from the article provide evidence that supports your answer to question 3?

_____9-10_____

_____4_____ Number of correct answers

Record your personal assessment of your work on the Critical Thinking Chart on page 74.

Personal Response

How do you think people who released J.J. felt when she finally headed out to sea?

_____

_____

_____

Self-Assessment

I'm proud of how I answered question # _____ in section _____ because

_____

_____

_____

_____

CRITICAL THINKING

NURSE HERO
Taking Charge at a Crash Site

It was a sound that those who heard will never forget. It was the sound of steel exploding on steel. What made it worse was that many people saw what was about to happen but could do nothing to stop it. The kids at the back of the school bus saw it coming. So did the engineer of the commuter express train. And so did the people in cars waiting at a railroad crossing in Fox River Grove, Illinois.

2   On October 25, 1995, a train weighing about 620 tons smashed into the back of a school bus. The train hit the bus with such force that it ripped the body of the vehicle off its chassis, spinning it around 180 degrees. The collision sent books, homework, and even a tiny teddy bear flying through the windows. Students, too, went crashing through the glass.

3   The accident occurred at about 7:20 A.M., when 35 students sat on the bus headed to the Cary-Grove High School. A substitute driver, unfamiliar with the bus route, was driving that day. She was running late; she had to ask students to help her with directions. When she arrived at the railroad tracks, she began to

The school bus chassis sits on the ground next to the railroad tracks the day after a train crashed into the bus, killing seven high school students.

drive across them. But the bus did not quite make it all the way across. Cars were backed up from a red traffic light not far away on the other side of the tracks. Some of the students laughed when the train crossing gate slammed down on the roof of the bus.

4   The smiles didn't last long. The students quickly realized that a closing gate meant a train was coming. When they saw the oncoming train, they panicked. Many ran for the front of the bus, screaming in terror. "The looks on those children's faces will never leave my mind," said one woman who was in a nearby car. "It was total fear."

5   "You could see the terror in their eyes," remembered Coreen Bachinsky, another witness.

6   Jim Homala, who was driving his own children to school, was parked behind the school bus. When he saw the train coming, he knew that it couldn't possibly stop in time. He recalled, "We started screaming, 'Go! Go!'"

7   When the train's engineer saw the back end of the bus on the tracks, he slammed on his emergency brake and blasted his horn. But it was too late. He couldn't stop his train in time. It was still going about 50 miles per hour when it hit the school bus. "It was over in a matter of seconds," said Homala.

8   "You could hear the metal, the glass flying, the screams. It was very, very scary," declared Bachinsky.

A memorial to the victims is set up at the railroad crossing where the deadly accident occurred.

9   "From then on out, all you heard was screaming," said Andrea Arens, who was standing nearby waiting for a train.

10   At that very moment, nurse Helen Getchell was pouring herself a cup of coffee at the White Hen Pantry on the other side of the train crossing. When she heard the crash, she froze for a second. The sound was like nothing Getchell had ever heard before. Then she put down her cup and rushed to the window. She saw what was left of the bus, and she saw bleeding kids lying on the ground.

11   "I just took off," Getchell later said. She raced across the road to the scene of the accident. Seeing the chaos, Getchell knew she had to get the rescue effort organized. She did so as calmly and quickly as she could.

12   "She immediately took charge," reported one eyewitness. First she called to the children still on the bus, telling them to get off if they could. Then Getchell, who had been a registered nurse for only 18 months, began barking orders to other people who came to the aid of the children. She told them to put pressure on the wounds of injured students to stop the bleeding. Getchell

herself went to work on the victims who appeared to be in the worst shape. "I just observed which kids needed the most help," she later said. Getchell noticed one boy who was badly injured. As she moved closer, she saw that he was beyond help. Grimly she moved on. She came to another boy, this one still alive. He was choking on his own blood. She knew she had to do something to clear his windpipe—and fast. "I needed suction, and there was absolutely nothing for me to work with," she remembered.

13   "Can somebody just go and get a suction?" she yelled.

14   Hearing her, Gail Rucker, the owner of the White Hen Pantry, thought of something that might help. She ordered someone to race back to the store to get a turkey baster. Getchell used it to suction out the boy's mouth. As she held him in her arms, she whispered to him, "'Breathe, honey, breathe!" She kept working until the boy's body went limp.

15   Later she tried to comfort the boy's parents. "He died in my arms," she said. "He didn't die by himself."

16   In all, seven children died in the crash and several others were badly injured. But

although Getchell couldn't save the most seriously injured, she was widely praised as a hero. She brought comfort to the frightened children. She directed volunteers as they arrived on the scene. And she bravely attempted to help those children most in need of assistance. In 1996, Helen Getchell became one of the first people ever to receive a special "Nurse Hero" award from the Red Cross and American Nurses Association. 🍂

If you have been timed while reading this article, enter your reading time below. Then turn to the Words-per-Minute Table on page 71 and look up your reading speed (words per minute). Enter your reading speed on the graph on page 72.

Reading Time: Lesson 2

3 : 32

Minutes   Seconds

A Finding the Main Idea

One statement below expresses the main idea of the article. One statement is too general, or too broad. The other statement explains only part of the article; it is too narrow. Label the statements using the following key:

M—Main Idea   **B—Too Broad**   **N—Too Narrow**

_M_   1. Nurse Helen Getchell heroically provided emergency medical treatment to the victims of a collision between a train and a school bus at a railroad crossing.

_B_   2. After terrible accidents, heroes often step in to help victims.

_N_   3. Helen Getchell had stopped for a cup of coffee at the White Hen Pantry when she heard the sound of the express train crashing into the school bus.

_15_   Score 15 points for a correct M answer.

_10_   Score 5 points for each correct B or N answer.

_25_   **Total Score:** Finding the Main Idea

B Recalling Facts

How well do you remember the facts in the article? Put an X in the box next to the answer that correctly completes each statement about the article.

1. The driver of the bus was
   - ☒ a. a substitute who was unfamiliar with the route.
   - ☐ b. not paying attention to traffic.
   - ☐ c. deaf.

2. The bus stayed on the tracks because
   - ☐ a. the closing gate had trapped it on the tracks.
   - ☐ b. it had stalled.
   - ☒ c. traffic ahead had been stopped by a red light.

3. At the time of the accident, Helen Getchell had been a registered nurse for
   - ☐ a. one month.
   - ☒ b. 18 months.
   - ☐ c. 18 years.

4. Helen Getchell performed all these activities except
   - ☐ a. comforting the frightened children.
   - ☒ b. driving the bus off the tracks.
   - ☐ c. directing the volunteers.

5. Helen Getchell received the
   - ☐ a. Volunteer of the Year award.
   - ☐ b. Medal of Honor.
   - ☒ c. Nurse Hero award.

Score 5 points for each correct answer.

_25_   **Total Score:** Recalling Facts

C | Making Inferences

When you combine your own experience and information from a text to draw a conclusion that is not directly stated in that text, you are making an inference. Below are five statements that may or may not be inferences based on information in the article. Label the statements using the following key:

C—Correct Inference   **F—Faulty Inference**

_F_ 1. The crash occurred in a rural area, far away from the city.

_C_ 2. Bus drivers accept an awesome responsibility when they agree to drive school buses.

_F_ 3. If you have medical training, you can save the life of every patient you treat.

_C_ 4. Gail Rucker was a creative and flexible thinker.

_F_ 5. Helen Getchell was the only person who tried to help the young victims of the crash.

Score 5 points for each correct answer.

_25_ **Total Score:** Making Inferences

D | Using Words Precisely

Each numbered sentence below contains an underlined word or phrase from the article. Following the sentence are three definitions. One definition is closest to the meaning of the underlined word. One definition is opposite or nearly opposite. Label those two definitions using the following key. Do not label the remaining definition.

C—Closest   **O—Opposite or Nearly Opposite**

1. The <u>collision</u> sent books, homework, and even a tiny teddy bear flying through the windows.

____ a. event

_O_ b. near miss

_C_ c. crash

2. When they saw the oncoming train, they <u>panicked</u>.

_C_ a. became terrified

____ b. shouted

_O_ c. remained calm

3. Seeing the <u>chaos</u>, Getchell knew she had to get the rescue effort organized.

_O_ a. harmony and peace

_C_ b. disorder

~~____~~ c. accident

4. <u>Grimly</u> she moved on.

O _C_ a. with many hesitations

X _O_ b. quickly

C ____ c. doggedly; in a determined way

5. She kept working until the boy's body went <u>limp</u>.

C _____ a. droopy

_____ b. rigid

X C _____ c. to sleep

_____ 9 Score 3 points for each correct C answer.

_____ 8 Score 2 points for each correct O answer.

_____ 17 **Total Score:** Using Words Precisely

Enter the four total scores in the spaces below, and add them together to find your Reading Comprehension Score. Then record your score on the graph on page 73.

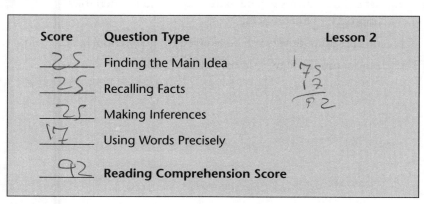

Score	Question Type	Lesson 2
25	Finding the Main Idea	
25	Recalling Facts	
25	Making Inferences	
17	Using Words Precisely	
92	**Reading Comprehension Score**	

Author's Approach

Put an X in the box next to the correct answer.

1. The author uses the first sentence of the article to

   ☒ a. appeal to the reader's curiosity about what caused the sound.

   ☐ b. compare the sound of a train and the sound of a bus.

   ☐ c. entertain the reader with a joke.

2. What does the author mean by the statement "When she [Helen Getchell] heard the crash, she froze for a second"?

   ☐ a. Getchell was too afraid for her own safety to move at all.

   ☐ b. Getchell became extremely cold for a few seconds.

   ☒ c. Getchell stopped moving while she tried to identify the sound she had just heard.

3. What is the author's purpose in writing "Nurse Hero: Taking Charge at a Crash Site"?

   ☐ a. To encourage the reader to avoid riding school buses

   ☒ b. To inform the reader about the heroic actions of Helen Getchell

   ☐ c. To emphasize the differences between bus drivers and nurses

4. What does the author imply by saying "As she moved closer, she [Getchell] saw that he [the injured boy] was beyond help"?

   ☐ a. The boy was not injured after all.

   ☒ b. The boy was already dead.

   ☐ c. Getchell couldn't reach the boy.

_____ 4 Number of correct answers

Record your personal assessment of your work on the Critical Thinking Chart on page 74.

Summarizing and Paraphrasing

Follow the directions provided for question 1. Put an X in the box next to the correct answer for question 2.

1. Reread paragraph 7 in the article. Below, write a summary of the paragraph in no more than 25 words.

   The Train crashed into the bus

   Reread your summary and decide whether it covers the important ideas in the paragraph. Next, decide how to shorten the summary to 15 words or less without leaving out any essential information. Write this summary below.

   same as above

2. Choose the best one-sentence paraphrase for the following sentence from the article:

   "The train hit the bus with such force that it ripped the body of the vehicle off its chassis, spinning it around 180 degrees."

   ☐ a. When the train hit the bus, the train spun around 180 degrees.

   ☒ b. The train crashed so strongly into the bus that bus's body ripped loose from the chassis and spun around to face the opposite direction.

   ☐ c. The train and the bus collided with such force that the bus spun around in a full circle.

  Number of correct answers

Record your personal assessment of your work on the Critical Thinking Chart on page 74.

Critical Thinking

Put an X in the box next to the correct answer for questions 1, 2, 4, and 5. Follow the directions provided for the other question.

1. Which of the following statements from the article is an opinion rather than a fact?

   ☐ a. "On October 25, 1995, a train weighing about 620 tons smashed into the back of a school bus."

   ☒ b. "It was very, very, very scary."

   ☐ c. "The accident occurred at about 7:20 A.M., when 35 students sat on the bus headed to the Cary-Grove High School."

2. From what the article told about the accident, you can predict that from now on

   ☒ a. school bus drivers will be extremely cautious when they approach railroad tracks.

   ☐ b. no substitute drivers will be allowed to drive school buses again.

   ☐ c. school buses will never cross railroad tracks.

3. Choose from the letters below to correctly complete the following statement. Write the letters on the lines.

According to the article, __b__ caused __a__ to back up, and the effect was __c__.

a. traffic

b. a red light

c. the school bus was stopped on the railroad tracks

4. Of the following theme categories, which would this story fit into?

☐ a. Mind your own business.

☐ b. Don't count on strangers to help you.

☒ c. Always be prepared.

5. What did you have to do to answer question 1?

☒ a. find an opinion (what someone thinks about something)

☐ b. find a description (how something looks)

☐ c. draw a conclusion (a sensible statement based on the text and your experience)

___5___ Number of correct answers

Record your personal assessment of your work on the Critical Thinking Chart on page 74.

Personal Response

If I were the author, I would add

_____

_____

_____

_____

because

_____

_____

_____

_____

Self-Assessment

When reading the article, I was having trouble with

_____

_____

_____

_____

CRITICAL THINKING

THE ANGEL OF LONG POINT

This drawing shows Abigail Becker holding the medal she received for her rescue of the men aboard the Conductor

Captain Henry Hackett sensed that a bad storm was brewing but hadn't arrived yet. It was November 23, 1854. With winter coming, Hackett knew that the sailing season was almost over. He figured it was now or never. He could take a chance sailing the three-masted schooner *Conductor* across Lake Erie from Amherstburg near Windsor to Toronto via the Welland Canal. Or he could let his cargo—8,000 bushels of corn—rot. He decided to go for it. As it turned out, Captain Hackett should have stayed put.

2 By early evening on November 24, a snowstorm had rolled in. Wind began whipping the snow into Hackett's face. Hackett was sailing nearly blind. He was only about halfway to his destination. He could not see Long Point, a thin peninsula sticking far out into Lake Erie from the Canadian side. He knew how treacherous the shallow waters were near Long Point. Hackett knew about the many sandbars and the fearsome undertows. But all he could do at that point was take down some of his sails and hope for the best.

3 Around midnight, Hackett's luck ran out. The *Conductor* ran into a sandbar a

half mile from Long Point and heeled over on its side. Huge lake waves battered the crippled ship. It took on so much water that the hull sank. Hackett and his crew had no choice but to climb up on the ship's rigging. There they lashed themselves to the masts so the wind would not blow them off. They could only hope that someone would see them before the waves destroyed the ship completely. If no one spotted them, they would have to swim for shore when the sun came up. That was a dim prospect. With the ice-cold water and strong undertows, even a good swimmer would be lucky to make it. In addition, the shifting sands underfoot made just wading difficult.

4   Hackett thought Long Point was uninhabited. Luckily for him and his crew, he was wrong. Abigail Becker, aged 23, lived there. She and her husband lived in a small cabin. They had several children, including six children from Mr. Becker's first marriage.

5   Early in the morning of November 25, Abigail awoke and built a fire in her kitchen. She had to make breakfast for the children. On that particular day, her husband was away. She went down to the beach to fetch a pail of fresh water. As she approached the beach, she saw a small, empty boat adrift. It was from the

Conductor. The boat had been washed off the deck during the night. Abigail had seen boats like this before and knew what it meant—a ship had run aground. Scanning the horizon, she spotted the men on the *Conductor*. Still lashed to the masts, they were hanging on for dear life.

6   Abigail realized that only she could rescue these men. No one else was around. Quickly, she mobilized the older children. "There is a vessel aground down the beach," she told them. "We must hurry if we are to help them." She and the children gathered wood to build a fire on the beach. That way, if Abigail could save the men, they could warm up when they came ashore. The children also brought blankets and a kettle for boiling tea. Then, although she couldn't swim a lick, Abigail waded out toward the men. She began to shout encouragement to the men of the *Conductor*, urging them to swim ashore.

7   Captain Hackett was the first to go. "If we remain here much longer," he told his men, "we are certain to be lost."

8   He kicked off his boots. "If I make shore successfully," he said, "the rest of you follow, one at a time."

9   With that, he plunged into the lake and started swimming for shore. Hackett was a strong swimmer. But the

powerful undertow and shifting sands beneath his feet soon sapped his strength. Abigail saw him start to drift farther away. Abigail splashed over to him and grabbed the collar of his coat. Somehow, she found the strength to pull him out of the water. She laid him next to the fire, and then she went back into the water to urge the next man to try to swim for shore.

10   The first mate, Jerome, went next. Like the captain, he swam well at first. But, also like the captain, the undertow soon

An artist's rendering of the medal Abigail Becker received.

swept him off his feet. He, too, began to drift away. Meanwhile, Hackett had regained some of his strength. When he saw Jerome struggling, he splashed back into the lake to get his mate. But he was far too weak to save anyone. Soon the two men clutched each other in a death-like grip while trying to stay afloat. They might have drowned each other if Abigail hadn't rushed out and dragged both away from the undertow.

11   One by one Abigail saved five other men in a similar manner. At one point, her lame stepson, Edward, tried to help her. His crutches, however, sank into the soft sand. Now Abigail had to rescue him as well as the man he had been trying to help. In the end, Abigail got everyone except the cook safely to shore. The cook couldn't swim and decided to stay lashed to the mast. There was nothing to do but leave him there until the next morning. Then, with the lake calmer, the men built a rough log raft and rescued the half-frozen, nearly dead cook.

12   After that daring rescue, Abigail become a Great Lakes legend. This "Angel of Long Point" was a hero to Canadians and Americans alike. Sailors and merchants collected a $550 reward to give to her. Queen Victoria sent her a personal letter along with $100. She also won a gold medal from the Benevolent Life Saving Association of New York.

13   Abigail Becker was no one-time hero. She saved six more shipwrecked sailors. She also saved a boy who had fallen down a well. Amazingly, Abigail Becker managed to fit in her heroism while raising 17 children! 🍃

If you have been timed while reading this article, enter your reading time below. Then turn to the Words-per-Minute Table on page 71 and look up your reading speed (words per minute). Enter your reading speed on the graph on page 72.

Reading Time: **Lesson 3**

_____3____ : ____58____

Minutes   *Seconds*

A | Finding the Main Idea

One statement below expresses the main idea of the article. One statement is too general, or too broad. The other statement explains only part of the article; it is too narrow. Label the statements using the following key:

M—Main Idea   **B—Too Broad**   **N—Too Narrow**

_B_ 1. Winter storms on Lake Erie can be dangerous, as sailors have discovered over the years.

_N_ 2. Abigail Becker lived with her husband and children in a cabin on Long Point.

_M_ 3. Abigail Becker rescued sailors who had been caught in an early winter storm near her home on Long Point.

___15___ Score 15 points for a correct M answer.

___10___ Score 5 points for each correct B or N answer.

___25___ **Total Score:** Finding the Main Idea

B | Recalling Facts

How well do you remember the facts in the article? Put an X in the box next to the answer that correctly completes each statement about the article.

1. Captain Hackett knew that if he didn't sail across Lake Erie immediately
   - ☐ a. he would not be home for Christmas.
   - ☒ b. his cargo would rot.
   - ☐ c. his crew would mutiny.

2. Long Point was
   - ☒ a. a peninsula.
   - ☐ b. an island.
   - ☐ c. a large city near the ocean.

3. Abigail Becker first guessed that a boat was in trouble when she
   - ☐ a. saw the *Conductor*'s crew lashed to the masts.
   - ☐ b. heard the distant cries of the sailors.
   - ☒ c. saw a small, empty boat adrift.

4. When the captain had trouble reaching the shore, Abigail
   - ☐ a. asked her children to rescue him.
   - ☒ b. waded into the water and pulled him to safety.
   - ☐ c. built a rough log raft to rescue him.

5. The only crew member that Abigail didn't save was the
   - ☐ a. captain.
   - ☐ b. first mate.
   - ☒ c. cook.

Score 5 points for each correct answer.

___25___ **Total Score:** Recalling Facts

C | Making Inferences

When you combine your own experience and information from a text to draw a conclusion that is not directly stated in that text, you are making an inference. Below are five statements that may or may not be inferences based on information in the article. Label the statements using the following key:

C—Correct Inference   F—Faulty Inference

_C___ 1. Abigail's son Edward was as brave and unselfish as his mother.

_F___ 2. Captain Hackett's cargo probably reached its destination in perfect condition.

_C___ 3. Abigail Becker was a person who was willing to take risks.

_F___ 4. In 1854, everyone who wanted to work on a boat on Lake Erie had to pass a swimming test.

_C___ 5. Captain Hackett and his crew were grateful to Abigail Becker and her family.

Score 5 points for each correct answer.

_25___ **Total Score:** Making Inferences

D | Using Words Precisely

Each numbered sentence below contains an underlined word or phrase from the article. Following the sentence are three definitions. One definition is closest to the meaning of the underlined word. One definition is opposite or nearly opposite. Label those two definitions using the following key. Do not label the remaining definition.

C—Closest   O—Opposite or Nearly Opposite

1. He knew how <u>treacherous</u> the shallow waters were near Long Point.

_____ a. beautiful

_C___ b. dangerous

_O___ c. safe

2. The *Conductor* ran into a sandbar a half mile from Long Point and <u>heeled</u> over on its side.

_C___ a. leaned

_____ b. sank

_O___ c. stood up straight

3. There they <u>lashed</u> themselves to the masts so the wind would not blow them off.

_O___ a. separated

_C___ b. tied

_____ c. compared

4. Quickly, she <u>mobilized</u> the older children.

_____ a. acted like

_O___ b. prevented from acting

_C___ c. put into action

5. But the powerful undertow and shifting sands beneath his feet soon <u>sapped</u> his strength.

___C___ a. drained away

_____ b. admired

___O___ c. built up

___15___ Score 3 points for each correct C answer.

___10___ Score 2 points for each correct O answer.

___25___ **Total Score:** Using Words Precisely

Enter the four total scores in the spaces below, and add them together to find your Reading Comprehension Score. Then record your score on the graph on page 73.

Score	Question Type	Lesson 3
_25_	Finding the Main Idea	
_25_	Recalling Facts	
_25_	Making Inferences	
_25_	Using Words Precisely	
_100_	**Reading Comprehension Score**	

Author's Approach

Put an X in the box next to the correct answer.

1. What does the author mean by the statement "Wind began whipping the snow into Hackett's face. Hackett was sailing nearly blind"?

☒ a. The blowing snow was so thick that Hackett could barely see where he was sailing.

☐ b. The blowing snow injured Hackett's eyes and made him nearly blind.

☐ c. The sunlight reflecting off the snow caused Hackett to have trouble seeing where he was going.

2. What is the author's purpose in writing "The Angel of Long Point"?

☐ a. To express an opinion about the importance of learning how to swim

☐ b. To inform the reader about shipping on the Great Lakes

☒ c. To describe a situation in which one person's heroism saved many lives

3. Judging by statements from the article "The Angel of Long Point," you can conclude that the author wants the reader to think that

☐ a. Captain Hackett always made good decisions.

☒ b. Abigail Becker was brave and heroic.

☐ c. Lake Erie can be dangerous in a storm.

4. Choose the statement below that is the weakest argument for taking a boat out on Lake Erie when a winter storm is coming.

☐ a. The boat's cargo will rot if you don't.

☒ b. If you do, the boat could run aground and sink in the storm.

☐ c. The boat could be trapped away from home port if you don't.

___3.5___ Number of correct answers

Record your personal assessment of your work on the Critical Thinking Chart on page 74.

Summarizing and Paraphrasing

Follow the directions provided for question 1. Put an X in the box next to the correct answer for question 2.

1. Look for the important ideas and events in paragraphs 9 and 10. Summarize those paragraphs in one or two sentences.

   Hackett could not swim across the water, but Abigail could. Jerome had similar issues but Abigail was the he...

2. Below are summaries of the article. Choose the summary that says all the most important things about the article but in the fewest words.

   ☐ a. Abigail Becker was willing to try to rescue travelers who needed her help near her home on Long Point.

   ☒ b. Captain Henry Hackett's boat ran aground near Long Point. Abigail Becker rescued all the crew members except the cook. Becker also proved her heroism in other situations and was called the "Angel of Long Point."

   ☐ c. Even though he knew a storm was coming, Captain Henry Hackett decided to take his boat filled with corn out onto Lake Erie. After his boat ran aground in a terrible storm, he and his crew lashed themselves to the masts and waited for someone to rescue them. When they were finally rescued, they were relieved.

   _1.5_ Number of correct answers

   Record your personal assessment of your work on the Critical Thinking Chart on page 74.

Critical Thinking

Put an X in the box next to the correct answer for questions 1, 3, and 4. Follow the directions provided for the other questions.

1. From what the article told about what happened to Captain Hackett's boat and crew, you can predict that Hackett will

   ☒ a. never again try to cross Lake Erie when he knows a storm is coming.

   ☐ b. continue to take his chances outrunning winter storms.

   ☐ c. never sail again.

2. Choose from the letters below to correctly complete the following statement. Write the letters on the lines.

   On the positive side, _a_, but on the negative side _c_.

   a. Abigail Becker saved the lives of the *Conductor*'s captain and crew

   b. Abigail Becker lived in a small cabin

   c. Captain Hackett's decision put many people in danger

3. What was the cause of the cook's unwillingness to leave the boat?

   ☒ a. He couldn't swim.

   ☐ b. He didn't trust Abigail Becker.

   ☐ c. He felt comfortable and happy on the boat.

4. If you were a captain on Lake Erie, how could you use the information in the article to keep your boat and crew safe?

   ☐ a. You could depend on other people to rescue you and your boat every time you run into trouble.

   ☐ b. You could sail near Long Point during bad storms.

   ☒ c. Unlike Captain Hackett, you could pay attention to the weather conditions and avoid sailing when bad weather is predicted.

5. In which paragraph did you find your information or details to answer question 3?

Paragraph 11

___5___ Number of correct answers

Record your personal assessment of your work on the Critical Thinking Chart on page 74.

Personal Response

What would you have done if you had been in Abigail Becker's place?

_____

_____

_____

_____

Self-Assessment

One of the things I did best when reading this article was

_____

_____

_____

_____

_____

I believe I did this well because

_____

_____

_____

_____

_____

THE WILD RIDE OF GEMINI 8

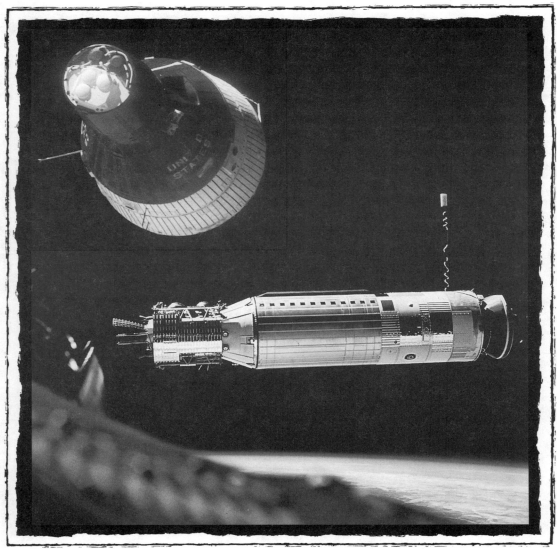

Agena *Target Docking vehicle as seen from* Gemini 8. *Inset photo (upper left):* Gemini 7 *photographed during a rendezvous with* Gemini 6, *went into space the year before* Gemini 8.

The mission looked like a roaring success. Everything was going as planned. On March 16, 1966, the U.S. spacecraft named *Gemini 8* linked up with another U.S. ship, the unmanned *Agena*. It was the first time in history that two spacecraft had been joined together while orbiting the earth. The docking went so well that astronauts Neil Armstrong and David Scott "[were] acting extremely 'ho-hum' about the whole thing," said one mission control official.

2   Armstrong and Scott soon began doing a series of special tests. These tests were essential for a trip to the moon planned for three years later. Scott first ordered the *Agena* to turn 180 degrees. This maneuver was done to see if both vehicles agreed on which way was down. "It worked quite well," radioed Armstrong. Scott gave 15 more orders to the *Agena*. All were successful. Then Scott asked the *Agena* to begin a series of gentle turns. Suddenly, something went terribly wrong. The *Agena*, with *Gemini 8* still linked to it, began to tumble wildly out of control.

3   At first, Armstrong thought the problem was with the *Agena*'s control system. He quickly ordered Scott to shut it down. Scott did so, but it didn't help. *Gemini 8* kept spinning at a faster and faster rate. Both astronauts knew they were in serious trouble. Unless the spacecraft could be brought under control, Scott and Armstrong would never make it back to earth alive.

4   No one knew it at the time, but the problem wasn't with the *Agena*'s control system. It was with one of *Gemini 8*'s 16 thrust rockets. The rockets were supposed to fire short blasts from time to time to keep the spaceship stable. But now the wires that controlled them had short-circuited. Rocket Number 8 was firing without command. At first it fired every three seconds, causing the spaceship to flip over end to end. Then it began firing continuously, making *Gemini* 8 tumble even faster.

5   To regain control of their own ship, the astronauts needed to break away from the *Agena*. But the normal undocking method would not work. The vehicles were spinning too fast. So in a last ditch effort, Armstrong fired *Gemini*'s own thruster rockets to release the *Agena*.

6   Armstrong hoped this move would stop the tumbling. But it didn't. After the *Agena* was unhooked, *Gemini*'s spinning just got worse. The ship was rolling over once every second. At that rate, the men were in danger of becoming totally disoriented. Even trained test pilots like Armstrong and Scott could not stand much more. "We've got serious problems here," radioed Armstrong to the command center. "We're tumbling end over end."

7   At that point, Armstrong made one last desperate move. He turned on a whole new set of rockets. These rockets, in the nose of the ship, were meant to be used only for reentering the earth's atmosphere. The gamble worked. Using his impressive flying skills, Armstrong was able to bring *Gemini 8* back to an even keel. "We are regaining control of the spacecraft slowly," he reported.

8   The astronauts now faced a new risk, however. They had to get *Gemini 8* back to earth at once. The reentry rockets had a limited supply of fuel, and they could not be shut off once they had been fired. So Armstrong had to work quickly. He had to get the ship into just the right angle for reentry before the fuel was gone. A wrong angle would cause the ship to burn up when it hit the earth's atmosphere.

9   If all went well, *Gemini 8* would land somewhere in the East China Sea. That was half a world away from where it had been scheduled to land in the Atlantic Ocean. It was also at least six hours away from the nearest U.S. Navy vessel. A 10-member rescue team rushed to Japan by plane. The team had two goals: first save

Astronauts David Scott (left) and Neil Armstrong wait to be picked up by the Navy after splashing down in the Pacific Ocean.

the crew, and then save the capsule. Rescuers planned to parachute down to *Gemini 8* after it splashed down. They would do everything they could to save the two astronauts. They also hoped to save the capsule from sinking by attaching a giant set of water wings to it.

10   To put their plan into action, the rescuers had to be at the right place at the right time. The ocean is huge. One slight miscalculation by the control center and the plane would miss *Gemini 8*'s splash-down point by several miles. If Armstrong even sneezed on the way down, he might nudge his ship far off course. The rescue team would have no radio guidance from Armstrong. His radio had to be shut off during reentry to conserve power.

11   As the time came for *Gemini 8* to reach earth, rescuers held their breath. Would the spacecraft survive reentry? If it did, would it come down where it was expected to? Would the rescue plane be able to find it? Les Schneider was the rescue plane's pilot. He strained his ears listening for the homing signal that the *Gemini* should have been sending out. At first he heard nothing. "Then there it was, a loud, clear signal," he later wrote. "Straight ahead. Now right. Now left. Now behind us....we had passed directly under the descending capsule." Moments later,

Schneider saw three orange and white parachutes bringing *Gemini 8* gently down. "I've got it," shouted Schneider over his radio. The media called it "the shout heard round the world."

12   Schneider banked his plane around and saw that *Gemini 8* was afloat. Rescue swimmers parachuted down to the bobbing capsule. In less than a minute they reached Armstrong and Scott. The two astronauts still inside the capsule heard human voices outside and then remembered to turn their radio back on. Their first words expressed some of the relief and happiness they felt. "*Gemini 8* here and are we glad to see you."

If you have been timed while reading this article, enter your reading time below. Then turn to the Words-per-Minute Table on page 71 and look up your reading speed (words per minute). Enter your reading speed on the graph on page 72.

Reading Time: Lesson 4

___3___ : ___17___

Minutes   Seconds

A | Finding the Main Idea

One statement below expresses the main idea of the article. One statement is too general, or too broad. The other statement explains only part of the article; it is too narrow. Label the statements using the following key:

M—Main Idea   **B—Too Broad**   **N—Too Narrow**

_B_   1. Humans' first ventures into space were filled with danger and heroism.

_N_   2. When *Gemini 8*'s thrust rockets began to fire continuously, the spacecraft started to spin out of control.

_M_   3. Cool heads, fast thinking, and the skill displayed by the pilots and the rescue team saved U.S. spacecraft *Gemini 8* from disaster.

_____ Score 15 points for a correct M answer.

_____ Score 5 points for each correct B or N answer.

_____ **Total Score:** Finding the Main Idea

B | Recalling Facts

How well do you remember the facts in the article? Put an X in the box next to the answer that correctly completes each statement about the article.

1. *Gemini 8* linked up with the *Agena* on
   - ☐ a.   March 16, 1996.
   - ☒ b.   March 16, 1966.
   - ☐ c.   April 16, 1946.

2. Pilot Neil Armstrong discovered that there was trouble when
   - ☒ a.   his spacecraft started to spin wildly.
   - ☐ b.   lights on his control panel flashed red.
   - ☐ c.   short-circuited wires began to send out sparks.

3. The problem was with
   - ☐ a.   *Gemini 8*'s reentry rockets.
   - ☐ b.   the *Agena*'s control panel.
   - ☒ c.   one of *Gemini 8*'s thrust rockets.

4. Armstrong brought *Gemini 8* under control by
   - ☒ a.   firing his reentry rockets.
   - ☐ b.   unhooking from the *Agena*.
   - ☐ c.   allowing *Gemini 8* to fall into the earth's atmosphere.

5. *Gemini 8* and its pilots were picked up in the
   - ☐ a.   Atlantic Ocean.
   - ☒ b.   East China Sea.
   - ☐ c.   Arctic Ocean.

Score 5 points for each correct answer.

_____ **Total Score:** Recalling Facts

C | Making Inferences

When you combine your own experience and information from a text to draw a conclusion that is not directly stated in that text, you are making an inference. Below are five statements that may or may not be inferences based on information in the article. Label the statements using the following key:

C—Correct Inference   **F—Faulty Inference**

___C___ 1. Astronauts are trained to be flexible and creative thinkers when they are under pressure.

___F___ 2. Thrust rocket number 8 was probably tampered with by someone who wanted to stop the mission.

___F___ 3. Neil Armstrong was a better pilot than David Scott was.

___C___ 4. When the reentry rockets were built, no one planned for them to be used to steady the ship while in space.

___F___ 5. It was only luck that caused the rescue team to be so close to *Gemini 8* when it splashed down.

Score 5 points for each correct answer.

_____ **Total Score:** Making Inferences

D | Using Words Precisely

Each numbered sentence below contains an underlined word or phrase from the article. Following the sentence are three definitions. One definition is closest to the meaning of the underlined word. One definition is opposite or nearly opposite. Label those two definitions using the following key. Do not label the remaining definition.

C—Closest   **O—Opposite or Nearly Opposite**

1. The rockets were supposed to fire short blasts from time to time to keep the spaceship <u>stable</u>.

   _____ a. comfortable

   ___C___ b. steady

   ___O___ c. wavering

2. Then it began firing <u>continuously</u>, making *Gemini 8* tumble even faster.

   ___O___ a. occasionally

   _____ b. strongly

   ___C___ c. constantly

3. At that rate, the men were in danger of becoming totally <u>disoriented</u>.

   _____ a. confused about their location

   ___C___ b. disabled

   ___O___ c. sure of themselves and their location

4. At that point, Armstrong made one last <u>desperate</u> move.

   _____ a. cautious

   ___O___ b. foolish

   ___C___ c. drastic

5. "...we had passed directly under the <u>descending</u> capsule."

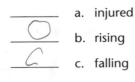

_____ a. injured

_____ b. rising

_____ c. falling

_____ Score 3 points for each correct C answer.

_____ Score 2 points for each correct O answer.

_____ **Total Score:** Using Words Precisely

Enter the four total scores in the spaces below, and add them together to find your Reading Comprehension Score. Then record your score on the graph on page 73.

Score	Question Type	Lesson 4
_____	Finding the Main Idea	
_____	Recalling Facts	
_____	Making Inferences	
_____	Using Words Precisely	
_____	**Reading Comprehension Score**	

Author's Approach

Put an X in the box next to the correct answer.

1. The main purpose of the first paragraph is to
   - ☐ a. explain the reasons for the U.S. space program.
   - ☐ b. compare Neil Armstrong and David Scott.
   - ☒ c. introduce the reader to the *Gemini 8* mission and its successes up to that point.

2. In this article, "If Armstrong even sneezed on the way down, he might nudge his ship far off course" means
   - ☐ a. If Armstrong's cold got any worse, he might have to land in an unknown area.
   - ☒ b. The ship's course could easily be altered; any slight, unplanned touch on the controls could change it.
   - ☐ c. The sound of Armstrong's sneeze could affect the working of the ship's controls.

3. The author probably wrote this article in order to
   - ☐ a. create a mood of terror.
   - ☐ b. raise money for the U.S. space program.
   - ☒ c. tell about an exciting rescue.

4. The author tells this story mainly by
   - ☒ a. telling about events in the order they happened.
   - ☐ b. comparing different topics.
   - ☐ c. using his or her imagination and creativity.

_____ Number of correct answers

Record your personal assessment of your work on the Critical Thinking Chart on page 74.

Summarizing and Paraphrasing

Follow the directions provided for questions 1 and 2. Put an X in the box next to the correct answer for question 3.

1. Complete the following one-sentence summary of the article using the lettered phrases from the phrase bank below. Write the letters on the lines.

> **Phrase Bank:**
> a. *Gemini 8*'s problems and how they were attacked
> b. the rescue of the pilots and the spacecraft at sea
> c. *Gemini 8*'s early successes

The article about "The Wild Ride of *Gemini 8*" begins with ___C___, goes on to explain ___a___, and ends with ___b___.

2. Reread paragraph 4 in the article. Below, write a summary of the paragraph in no more than 25 words.

Gemini 8 was causing the tumbling.

Reread your summary and decide whether it covers the important ideas in the paragraph. Next, decide how to shorten the summary to 15 words or less without leaving out any essential information. Write this summary below.

Same as above

3. Choose the sentence that correctly restates the following sentence from the article:

"The reentry rockets had a limited supply of fuel, and they could not be shut off once they had been fired."

☐ a. Although the reentry rockets had little fuel, they could be shut off after they had been fired once.

☒ b. Because there was only so much fuel available for the reentry rockets, they couldn't be shut off once they were fired.

☐ c. Once fired, the reentry rockets couldn't be shut off; in addition, their fuel supply was limited.

_____ Number of correct answers

Record your personal assessment of your work on the Critical Thinking Chart on page 74.

Critical Thinking

Follow the directions provided for questions 1 and 3. Put an X in the box next to the correct answer for the other questions.

1. For each statement below, write O if it expresses an opinion or write F if it expresses a fact.

____F____ a. When *Gemini 8* and the *Agena* linked in space, it was the first time in history that two spacecraft had joined while orbiting the earth.

____O____ b. No one should risk human lives on dangerous ventures such as space travel.

____F____ c. Rocket Number 8 started firing continuously, flipping the ship over and over.

2. Judging by the events in the article, you can predict that the following will happen next:

☐ a. The pilots will admit that they made mistakes that almost cost their lives.

☒ b. The pilots and the rescue team will congratulate each other.

☐ c. The pilots will be punished by space program officials.

3. Using what you know about *Gemini 8* and what is told about the *Agena* in the article, name three ways *Gemini 8* is similar to and three ways *Gemini 8* is different from the *Agena*. Cite the paragraph number(s) where you found details in the article to support your conclusions.

Similarities

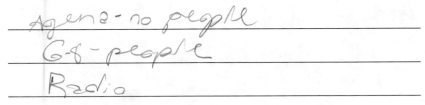

Space ship

Controls

orbited

Differences

Agena - no people

G-8 - people

Radio

4. If you were an astronaut, how could you use the information in the article to make your space mission a success?

☐ a. Like the *Gemini 8* pilots, act like your mission is "extremely 'ho-hum.'"

☐ b. Like Neil Armstrong, use the reentry rockets to keep the ship steady.

☒ c. Like Neil Armstrong, study all the parts of your spacecraft and know what each part can and can't do.

_____ Number of correct answers

Record your personal assessment of your work on the Critical Thinking Chart on page 74.

Personal Response

A question I would like answered by astronaut Neil Armstrong is

_____

_____

_____

Self-Assessment

Which concepts or ideas from the article were difficult to understand?

_____

_____

_____

Which were easy to understand?

_____

_____

CRITICAL THINKING

SAVED FROM A MOB

The verdict was in. On April 29, 1992, the police officers were found not guilty. After seeing a graphic videotape showing four white policemen beating a black man named Rodney King, the jury said the officers had done nothing wrong. The verdict outraged African Americans. Within minutes, young blacks started to seek some sort of revenge. They began to riot in the streets of south-central Los Angeles. They pelted cars and trucks with bricks and bottles. In a few cases, they attacked the drivers personally.

2   Gregory Alan-Williams, an African-American TV actor, heard the news over his car radio. As he listened, something inside him stirred. He knew what it was like to be the victim of a senseless crime. Twenty-three years earlier he had been viciously attacked by a white boy in his high school. Other students had just watched and laughed. "I know what it's like to be a victim of a mob and not know why," he said later. "It's probably the most helpless and hopeless situation anyone can be in."

Television actor Gregory Alan-Williams testifies at a trial following the 1992 riots in Los Angeles. Alan-Williams helped save the life of a man who was senselessly beaten by the rioters.

3   And so despite the risks involved, Alan-Williams rushed to the scene. He reached the corner of Florence and Normandie Avenues near dusk. He could see the rioters hurling bottles and bricks at passing cars. Some also had metal bars. As long as the drivers did not slow down or stop, they could get past the angry mob. But then Alan-Williams saw a brown Ford Bronco stop. "Grave mistake," he thought to himself.

4   The driver of the Bronco was Takao Hirata, a Japanese American. One member of the mob stepped forward and demanded Hirata's money. Hirata gave up his wallet. But the rioters wanted more than cash. They were angry, and they needed a target for their anger. Hirata looked like the perfect victim.

5   Sensing that he was in trouble, Hirata leaned over and locked his doors. Just then, one of the youths broke the window with a rod. Then a bottle smashed against Hirata's skull. The rioters began to punch him in the face. Within just a

few seconds, they had knocked him unconscious.

6   At that point, Alan-Williams waded into the mob. The rioters were about to open the door of the Bronco. They wanted to drag Hirata out so they could all beat him more. "Come on," pleaded Alan-Williams, "y'all know this [isn't] right." His plea fell on deaf ears.

7   Luckily, at that moment two of the rioters began to fight with each other. That gave Alan-Williams a chance to act. He grabbed Hirata and tried to lift him out

Demonstrators protest the acquittal of four police officers charged with beating Rodney King.

48

of the car. But Hirata was quite heavy and hard to move. "Come on, man. Let's go," he cried. At last, Alan-Williams was able to pull Hirata out of the car. As he did so, a second bottle shattered against Hirata's head, sending shards into Alan-William's face.

8   Alan-Williams dragged Hirata away from the mob. As he paused to rest, he felt the injured man begin to stir. "Can you walk?" he asked. Hirata slowly shook his head. "Well, you've got to walk or you're going to die," warned Alan-Williams.

9   Hirata struggled to his feet. He put an arm around his rescuer's neck. Slowly, the pair moved down the street. Alan-Williams tried to shield Hirata's face. He didn't want other rioters to see that Hirata was Asian. Still, more bricks and bottles bounced around the two men. An elderly black woman saw what was happening from her front porch and asked if she should call 911. "Please," said Alan-Williams gratefully.

10   At last, a police patrol car pulled up. Alan-Williams said, "This guy's hurt bad and needs help." But the two officers, a black man and a white woman, took a look and drove off without saying a word. "I couldn't believe it," said Alan-Williams. "I had been certain that eventually, in the midst of this madness, I would run into a

cop…. Now I watched the help I'd counted on drive away."

11   Luckily, though, help did arrive. An African-American man pulled up in a van. "Yo, man," the driver shouted, "you want me to take him to the hospital?"

12   After all that had just happened, Alan-Williams was afraid to turn Hirata over to a black man. "Naw…that's all right," he said.

13   But he quickly changed his mind. Blood was dripping out of Hirata's ears. He could be dying for all Alan-Williams knew. Alan-Williams decided he had no choice. He had to trust the driver. "You're going to take him to the hospital, right?"

14   "For real, brother," the driver assured him. The two men lifted Hirata into the van. Finally, after watching the driver speed off to the hospital with Hirata, Alan-Williams went home to his wife and four children.

15   Takao Hirata survived the attack. But he had all his front teeth knocked out. Also, his face was severely cut and badly bruised. A few days later, Alan-Williams went to Hirata's home. Hirata struggled to his feet to welcome his rescuer. The two men embraced. Then Hirata gave Alan-Williams a special gift. It was a miniature samurai helmet. "*You* are my samurai," Hirata said.

16   For his part, Hirata felt no racial hatred toward African Americans. He had grown up not far from where the mob assaulted him. "[The people who attacked me] were thugs," he said. "[They were not] regular people."

17   To many, Gregory Alan-Williams was a hero. But the actor shrugged off such claims. "It was selfish," he said of his brave act. "If I don't help this man, when the mob comes for me, there will be nobody there for me." Alan-Williams added, "If I stood there and watched this man be murdered, then what sort of justice could I ask for myself?"

If you have been timed while reading this article, enter your reading time below. Then turn to the Words-per-Minute Table on page 71 and look up your reading speed (words per minute). Enter your reading speed on the graph on page 72.

Reading Time: Lesson 5
4 : 43
Minutes   Seconds

A | Finding the Main Idea

One statement below expresses the main idea of the article. One statement is too general, or too broad. The other statement explains only part of the article; it is too narrow. Label the statements using the following key:

M—Main Idea   B—Too Broad   N—Too Narrow

_B_ 1. It is difficult to stand up to an angry mob.

_M_ 2. Gregory Alan-Williams risked his own safety to successfully rescue an innocent man who was being attacked by a mob.

_N_ 3. Gregory Alan-Williams had been the victim of a senseless crime when he was only a teenager.

_____ Score 15 points for a correct M answer.

_____ Score 5 points for each correct B or N answer.

_____ **Total Score:** Finding the Main Idea

B | Recalling Facts

How well do you remember the facts in the article? Put an X in the box next to the answer that correctly completes each statement about the article.

1. The attack on Takao Hirata took place in
   ☐ a. Chicago.
   ☐ b. New York City.
   ☒ c. Los Angeles.

2. The mob picked on Hirata because he
   ☒ a. stopped.
   ☐ b. had been involved in the beating of Rodney King.
   ☐ c. refused to give them his wallet.

3. Alan-Williams pulled Hirata out of his car when
   ☒ a. two rioters started to fight each other.
   ☐ b. the police arrived.
   ☐ c. someone stopped and offered to drive Hirata to the hospital.

4. Hirata gave Alan-Williams a
   ☐ a. silver sword.
   ☒ b. miniature samurai helmet.
   ☐ c. cash reward for saving his life.

5. Hirata had grown up in
   ☐ a. Japan.
   ☒ b. Los Angeles.
   ☐ c. China.

Score 5 points for each correct answer.

_____ **Total Score:** Recalling Facts

C | Making Inferences

When you combine your own experience and information from a text to draw a conclusion that is not directly stated in that text, you are making an inference. Below are five statements that may or may not be inferences based on information in the article. Label the statements using the following key:

C—Correct Inference   **F—Faulty Inference**

_C_ 1. The mob might not have beaten Hirata if he had been African American instead of Japanese American.

_F_ 2. Alan-Williams did not know that he was walking into a dangerous situation when he went to south-central Los Angeles that night.

_C_ 3. Hirata was grateful to Alan-Williams for his help.

_F_ 4. Police maintained perfect control over the Los Angeles streets at all times during this situation.

_F_ 5. Most African Americans in Los Angeles participated in the riots after the Rodney King verdict.

Score 5 points for each correct answer.

_____ **Total Score:** Making Inferences

D | Using Words Precisely

Each numbered sentence below contains an underlined word or phrase from the article. Following the sentence are three definitions. One definition is closest to the meaning of the underlined word. One definition is opposite or nearly opposite. Label those two definitions using the following key. Do not label the remaining definition.

C—Closest   **O—Opposite or Nearly Opposite**

1. Despite a <u>graphic</u> videotape showing four white policemen beating a black man named Rodney King, the jury said the officers had done nothing wrong.

_____ a. vivid and plainly shown

_O_ b. hard to understand

_C_ c. cruel

2. Alan-Williams tried to <u>shield</u> Hirata's face.

_____ a. see

_O_ b. expose

_C_ c. hide

3. It was a <u>miniature</u> samurai helmet.

_C_ a. tiny

_O_ b. huge

_____ c. old

4. He had grown up not far from where the mob had <u>assaulted</u> him.

_C_ a. attacked

_O_ b. defended

_____ c. brought

5. "[The people who attacked me] were <u>thugs</u>," he said.

_____ a. angry

_____ b. honest citizens

_____ c. criminals

_____ Score 3 points for each correct C answer.

_____ Score 2 points for each correct O answer.

_____ **Total Score:** Using Words Precisely

Enter the four total scores in the spaces below, and add them together to find your Reading Comprehension Score. Then record your score on the graph on page 73.

Score	Question Type	Lesson 5
_____	Finding the Main Idea	
_____	Recalling Facts	
_____	Making Inferences	
_____	Using Words Precisely	
_____	**Reading Comprehension Score**	

Author's Approach

Put an X in the box next to the correct answer.

1. The main purpose of the first paragraph is to

☒ a. describe the time and place of the events to follow.

☐ b. express an opinion about the people who rioted.

☐ c. compare white and black Americans.

2. What is the author's purpose in writing "Saved from a Mob"?

☐ a. To entertain the reader with a sad story

☐ b. To inform the reader about the 1992 riots in Los Angeles

☒ c. To describe a situation in which one man bravely rescued another

3. From the statements below, choose those that you believe the author would agree with.

☐ a. Gregory Alan-Williams should have minded his own business.

☒ b. People involved in a riot can become cruel and dangerous.

☒ c. Gregory Alan-Williams was a real hero.

_____ Number of correct answers

Record your personal assessment of your work on the Critical Thinking Chart on page 74.

Summarizing and Paraphrasing

Follow the directions provided for question 1. Put an X in the box next to the correct answer for the other questions.

1. Complete the following one-sentence summary of the article using the lettered phrases from the phrase bank below. Write the letters on the lines.

> **Phrase Bank:**
> a. Alan-Williams's explanation for his actions
> b. the verdict in the Rodney King case
> c. how Alan-Williams rescued Takao Hirata

The article about Gregory Alan-Williams begins with __b__, goes on to explain __c__, and ends with __a__.

2. Below are summaries of the article. Choose the summary that says all the most important things about the article but in the fewest words.

☐ a. After police officers were found not guilty in Rodney King's beating, members of the Los Angeles African-American community rioted in protest. Gregory Alan-Williams rescued an innocent victim, Takao Hirata, from the angry mob. Hirata showed his gratitude with a small gift.

☒ b. Alan-Williams was a brave man who willingly entered an area of unrest to rescue an innocent victim, Takao Hirata.

☐ c. Gregory Alan-Williams had hoped to get some help from the Los Angeles police. That's why he was amazed when a patrol car carrying a black police man and a white police woman passed up both him and his injured companion.

3. Read the statement about the article below. Then read the paraphrase of that statement. Choose the reason that best tells why the paraphrase does not say the same thing as the statement.

Statement: As long as the drivers did not slow down or stop, they could get past the angry mob.

Paraphrase: There was no way to get past the angry mob, even if you were in a locked car.

☐ a. Paraphrase says too much.

☐ b. Paraphrase doesn't say enough.

☒ c. Paraphrase doesn't agree with the statement about the article.

> _____ Number of correct answers
>
> Record your personal assessment of your work on the Critical Thinking Chart on page 74.

Critical Thinking

Put an X in the box next to the correct answer for questions 1 and 4. Follow the directions provided for the other questions.

1. Which of the following statements from the article is an opinion rather than a fact?

☒ a. "On April 29, 1992, the police officers were found not guilty."

☐ b. "[The people who attacked me] were thugs," he said. [They were not] regular people."

☐ c. "The driver of the Bronco was Takao Hirata, a Japanese American."

2. Choose from the letters below to correctly complete the following statement. Write the letters on the lines.

In the article, ___b___ and ___C___ are alike with regard to their race.

a.   Takao Hirata

b.   Gregory Alan-Williams

c.   the rioters

3. Read paragraph 1. Then choose from the letters below to correctly complete the following statement. Write the letters on the lines.

According to paragraph 1, ___C___ happened because ___b___.

a.   African Americans were outraged at the Rodney King verdict

b.   Gregory Alan-Williams had been attacked by a white boy

c.   the riots in Los Angeles in April 1992

4. How is the story of Gregory Alan-Williams related to the theme of this book?

☐ a.   The police officers of Los Angeles disappointed Gregory Alan-Williams when he needed help.

☐ b.   Gregory Alan-Williams had once been a victim himself.

☒ c.   Gregory Alan-Williams saved the life of Takao Hirata by pulling him away from an angry mob.

_____ Number of correct answers

Record your personal assessment of your work on the Critical Thinking Chart on page 74.

Personal Response

Would you recommend this article to other students? Explain.

_____

_____

_____

_____

Self-Assessment

I was confused on question # _____ in section _____ because

_____

_____

_____

_____

IDA LEWIS TO THE RESCUE

On a cool and windy September day in 1858, Ida Lewis stood at the door of the Lime Rock lighthouse in Newport, Rhode Island. Glancing across the bay toward Fort Adams, she noticed four boys sailing in a strange way. They seemed unsure of where they were going, so Ida kept a close eye on them. As she watched, one of the boys shinnied up the mast and rocked the boat back and forth, laughing as he did so. Ida knew the boat could not handle that kind of roughhousing. She was right. A few moments later the boat tipped over, spilling the four boys out into the cold water of the Atlantic Ocean.

2   Ida knew the boys could never make it to shore on their own, nor could they get their boat upright again. Quickly she dashed to the boat house. She slid the lifeboat down into the water and rowed out to the boys. Panicked, they tried to grab at the side of her lifeboat. To keep them from capsizing her boat, she wisely avoided them until she had rowed into just the right position. Then, one by one, she pulled them over the stern and into the boat. Back on shore, she gave each shivering boy a strong dose of hot molasses.

3   That was not a bad day's work for a 16-year-old girl. But then again, Ida was no ordinary teenager. She could row a boat better than almost anyone else her own age. And she was, without doubt, the best swimmer in the entire town of Newport.

Ida Lewis sits in her rowboat, the Rescue, *as her dog looks on near the Lime Rock Lighthouse in Newport, Rhode Island.*

Beyond that, Ida had an important job. Her father, Captain Hosea Lewis, had been the Lime Rock lighthouse keeper for four years. But he had recently suffered a massive stroke which left him unable to work. To make things worse, Ida's sister had fallen gravely ill. With her mother busy taking care of the two invalids, Ida was left to run the lighthouse alone. It was a job she would hold for the next 54 years. During that time, she was credited with rescuing at least 18 people. She became known as "the heroine of Lime Rock."

4   For a long time, no one knew about Ida's exploits. She was far too modest to tell anyone. For her, saving lives was no big deal—it was just part of her job. The folks she saved often failed to spread the word. Those four boys, for example, were too embarrassed to tell their parents that a girl had saved them from drowning. That story didn't become known for many years.

5   Often, Ida Lewis didn't even get a "thank you" for her efforts. That was the case with the Civil War veteran she saved in 1866. Three soldiers who were stationed at Fort Adams spent the evening in a Newport bar. They needed to get back to the fort before dawn. As they stumbled along the shore toward the fort, they spotted an unattended skiff. It was a long walk back to Fort Adams but just a short row across the bay. So the soldiers stole the skiff and took the shortcut.

6   One of the men sat in the stern while the other two handled the oars. For some reason, one of the oarsmen began pounding his foot on the bottom of the skiff. Before long, he punched a hole in it. As the boat sank, he and the other oarsman began swimming for shore. They were never heard from again; whether

The Lime Rock Lighthouse in Newport Harbor, Newport, Rhode Island, around 1900

they drowned or made it safely to shore remains a mystery. But the man in the stern stayed behind, clinging desperately to the damaged skiff.

7   Ida, who had heard his frantic screams, rowed quickly to the rescue. The man was far too heavy for Ida to lift into the lifeboat. There was only one thing she could do. She tied a rope under the man's armpits and lashed him to the side of the boat. Then she rowed slowly back to the shore.

8   Once safely back in the lighthouse, Ida revived the man. Then she lent him some of her little brother's clothes. The man accepted these gifts without saying a word. Later, when he felt strong enough, he simply got up and left without speaking to Ida. He never returned the clothes, either. All Ida got for her troubles was a badly wrenched back that would bother her for the rest of her life.

9   Ida finally began to get recognition for her heroism in 1867. That was when she made her most unusual rescue. Three men were walking a valuable sheep along the streets of Newport on a frigid winter morning. Without warning the sheep bolted, scurried out onto the Old Mill Wharf, and plunged headfirst into the bay. A powerful gale blew the animal farther and farther out to sea. The men jumped into a boat and rowed after their prize sheep. The boat was too small to fit all three of them; when a large wave hit, the boat capsized.

10   Ida, who had been sewing by her window, saw what happened. Draping a cape over her shoulder, she rushed to the scene. As she approached the drowning men, she had to laugh. Despite their own chances of drowning, they were still yelling about the sheep. Ida calmly pulled each one into her boat and rowed them to safety. Once they were deposited on shore, she rowed back out into the fierce storm and rescued the poor sheep. The three men thanked her profusely. And, unlike previous people she had saved, they praised Ida to everyone within earshot.

11   Captain Lewis agreed that his daughter was a marvel. He praised her ability to handle the turbulent sea. He once said, "She knew how to handle a boat, hold onto wind, and fight a gale better than any man I ever saw wet an oar, and do it, too, when the sea was breaking over her."

12   As Ida's fame spread, she continued to watch out for people in trouble. In 1869, two solders from Fort Adams went sailing with a young boatman. In the icy March waters, the boatman—really just a boy—apparently got lost. The boat drifted into choppy waters and overturned. This time Ida, who had been sick in bed with a cold, couldn't save them all. The boy drowned. But with help from her little brother, Ida saved the two soldiers.

13   One of the soldiers told his story to *The New York Herald Tribune*. Before long, Ida Lewis was a true celebrity. Many papers published stories of her rescues. *Harper's Weekly*, a leading magazine of the time, put her on their cover. Ida even inspired songs such as the "Rescue Polka." Susan B. Anthony praised her for helping women gain equality. Ida won a special medal from Congress for her work. Famous people dropped by the Lime Rock lighthouse just to say hello. Once, in 1869, President Ulysses S. Grant paid a visit. As he stepped out of the boat, the President got his feet wet. "I have come to see Ida Lewis," Grant laughed, "and to see her I'd get wet up to my armpits, if necessary."

14   Ida made her last rescue in 1904 at the age of 62. A friend fell overboard while rowing out to see her. Ida, still strong, ran to her lifeboat and rescued the friend.

15   In the fall of 1911, Ida became seriously ill. On October 24, the soldiers at Fort Adams were holding artillery practice. But when they learned that Ida was sick in bed, they stopped firing their cannons. They wanted to show their respect for "the heroine of Lime Rock." The next day, Ida Lewis died peacefully in bed at the age of 69. At her funeral, Reverend Stanley C. Hughes called her "the most remarkable woman Newport has ever produced." 🍃

If you have been timed while reading this article, enter your reading time below. Then turn to the Words-per-Minute Table on page 71 and look up your reading speed (words per minute). Enter your reading speed on the graph on page 72.

Reading Time: Lesson 6

___4___ : ___43___
Minutes   Seconds

A | Finding the Main Idea

One statement below expresses the main idea of the article. One statement is too general, or too broad. The other statement explains only part of the article; it is too narrow. Label the statements using the following key:

M—Main Idea   **B—Too Broad**   **N—Too Narrow**

_M_ 1. Ida Lewis is credited with rescuing at least 18 people from the sea over the years in which she served as lighthouse keeper in Newport, Rhode Island.

_B_ 2. Ida Lewis was a courageous woman.

_N_ 3. Ida Lewis became famous after one person she rescued told his story to *The New York Herald Tribune*.

_____	Score 15 points for a correct M answer.
_____	Score 5 points for each correct B or N answer.
_____	**Total Score:** Finding the Main Idea

B | Recalling Facts

How well do you remember the facts in the article? Put an X in the box next to the answer that correctly completes each statement about the article.

1. Ida Lewis assumed the job of lighthouse keeper after
   - ☐ a. she left home.
   - ☐ b. she filled out an application and was chosen for the job.
   - ☒ c. her father suffered a stroke.

2. In 1866, three Civil War veterans
   - ☒ a. stole a skiff and then punched a hole in its bottom.
   - ☐ b. told *The New York Herald Tribune* about Ida Lewis's courage.
   - ☐ c. rowed into the ocean to catch a prize sheep.

3. Ida Lewis was lighthouse keeper for
   - ☐ a. 16 years.
   - ☒ b. 54 years.
   - ☐ c. 69 years.

4. After Ida rescued a Civil War veteran, he
   - ☐ a. thanked her profusely.
   - ☐ b. wrote a song about her.
   - ☒ c. left without saying a word of thanks to her.

5. Ida Lewis was rewarded for her bravery with a
   - ☐ a. raise in pay.
   - ☐ b. new boat.
   - ☒ c. special medal from Congress.

	Score 5 points for each correct answer.
_____	**Total Score:** Recalling Facts

C | Making Inferences

When you combine your own experience and information from a text to draw a conclusion that is not directly stated in that text, you are making an inference. Below are five statements that may or may not be inferences based on information in the article. Label the statements using the following key:

C—Correct Inference   **F—Faulty Inference**

___C___ 1. Ida Lewis spent a great deal of time observing the ocean and the people who were sailing by the lighthouse.

___F___ 2. Ida Lewis charged a fee for rescuing careless sailors.

___F___ 3. Sheep instinctively know how to swim.

___F___ 4. Congress gives out medals only to members of the military forces.

___C___ 5. Ida Lewis was not aware that many people admired her.

Score 5 points for each correct answer.

_____ **Total Score:** Making Inferences

D | Using Words Precisely

Each numbered sentence below contains an underlined word or phrase from the article. Following the sentence are three definitions. One definition is closest to the meaning of the underlined word. One definition is opposite or nearly opposite. Label those two definitions using the following key. Do not label the remaining definition.

C—Closest   **O—Opposite or Nearly Opposite**

1. With her mother busy taking care of the two <u>invalids</u>, Ida was left to run the lighthouse alone.

   ___C___ a. sick people

   ___O___ b. healthy people

   _____ c. unusual people

2. As they stumbled along the shore toward the fort, they spotted an <u>unattended</u> skiff.

   _____ a. small

   ___C___ b. alone

   ___O___ c. closely guarded

3. The three men thanked her <u>profusely</u>.

   ___O___ a. barely enough

   _____ b. loudly

   ___C___ c. abundantly

4. He praised her ability to handle the <u>turbulent</u> sea.

   ___O___ a. calm and peaceful

   ___C___ b. rough and unsettled

   _____ c. green and sparkling

5. Before long, Ida Lewis was a true <u>celebrity</u>.

_____ a. unknown person

_____ b. holy person

_____ c. famous person

_____ Score 3 points for each correct C answer.

_____ Score 2 points for each correct O answer.

_____ **Total Score:** Using Words Precisely

Enter the four total scores in the spaces below, and add them together to find your Reading Comprehension Score. Then record your score on the graph on page 73.

Score	Question Type	Lesson 6
_____	Finding the Main Idea	
_____	Recalling Facts	
_____	Making Inferences	
_____	Using Words Precisely	
_____	**Reading Comprehension Score**	

Author's Approach

Put an X in the box next to the correct answer.

1. The author uses the first sentence of the article to

☒ a. inform the reader about the setting of the article.

☐ b. describe the personality of Ida Lewis.

☐ c. compare September with other times of the year.

2. Which of the following statements from the article best describes Ida Lewis's seamanship?

☐ a. "All Ida got for her troubles was a badly wrenched back that would bother her for the rest of her life."

☒ b. "'She knew how to handle a boat, hold onto wind, and fight a gale better than any man I ever saw wet an oar, and do it, too, when the sea was breaking over her.'"

☐ c. "Back on shore, she gave each shivering boy a strong dose of hot molasses."

3. Judging by statements from the article "Ida Lewis to the Rescue," you can conclude that the author wants the reader to think that

☐ a. Ida Lewis was willing to step in and act with courage wherever she was needed.

☐ b. Ida Lewis resented not getting much recognition for her rescue efforts early in her life.

☒ c. Ida Lewis was an extraordinary human being.

4. Choose the statement below that is the weakest argument for admiring Ida Lewis.

☐ a. Ida Lewis rescued many people from almost certain death.

☐ b. Ida Lewis was willing to help people even though she put herself at risk.

☒ c. Ida Lewis's picture appeared on the cover of a magazine.

_____ Number of correct answers

Record your personal assessment of your work on the Critical Thinking Chart on page 74.

Summarizing and Paraphrasing

Follow the directions provided for question 1. Put an X in the box next to the correct answer for question 2.

1. Look for the important ideas and events in paragraphs 10 and 11. Summarize those paragraphs in one or two sentences.

She was finally recognized

2. Choose the best one-sentence paraphrase for the following sentence from the article:

"They [the men] were never heard from again; whether they drowned or made it safely to shore remains a mystery."

☒ a. No one ever found out what happened to the men—whether they reached shore safely or drowned.

☐ b. It was later discovered that the two men, who people thought had drowned, had actually made it safely to shore.

☐ c. No one knows or cares whether the men made it safely to shore or drowned.

_____ Number of correct answers

Record your personal assessment of your work on the Critical Thinking Chart on page 74.

Critical Thinking

Follow the directions provided for questions 1, 3, and 4. Put an X in the box next to the correct answer for question 2.

1. For each statement below, write O if it expresses an opinion or write F if it expresses a fact.

_F_ a. Four boys saved by Ida Lewis were too embarrassed to tell their parents that a girl had rescued them.

_O_ b. Ida Lewis was the bravest person ever born in Newport, Rhode Island.

_F_ c. Ida Lewis died in bed at the age of 69.

2. From the article, you can predict that if Ida Lewis had never received any public recognition for her work, she would have

☐ a. stopped risking her life to rescue people.

☑ b. continued to rescue people anyway.

☐ c. given her story to the newspapers and magazines herself.

3. Think about cause-effect relationships in the article. Fill in the blanks in the cause-effect chart, drawing from the letters below.

Cause	Effect
Ida Lewis's father had a stroke.	*She was lighthousekeeper*
Three soldiers wanted to get back to Fort Adams quickly.	*stole boat*
men chased sheep	Ida Lewis laughed at the men.

a. They stole a skiff.

b. Three men were more concerned about their sheep than their own lives.

c. Ida Lewis took on the job of lighthouse keeper.

4. Which paragraphs from the article provide evidence that supports your answer to question 3?

_*108 11*_

_____ Number of correct answers

Record your personal assessment of your work on the Critical Thinking Chart on page 74.

Personal Response

If you could ask the author of the article one question, what would it be?

_____

_____

_____

_____

Self-Assessment

From reading this article, I have learned

_____

_____

_____

_____

CRITICAL THINKING

SAVING JEWS FROM THE NAZIS

A sidewalk café in Marseilles, France, around the time Varian Fry was there helping writers and artists escape from the Nazis

Varian Fry knew trouble was coming. Adolf Hitler and his Nazi party had taken control of Germany in 1933. Now they had begun a brutal campaign of persecuting the Jews. Fry saw this for himself when he was visiting Germany in 1935. Again and again, Fry, a writer from New York City, saw how the Nazis went after Jews. He saw bloody riots staged against them. Once he saw a Nazi soldier pin an old Jewish man's hand to a table with a knife. Then the Nazi pulled out the knife and walked away, laughing. After that, Fry, who was not a Jew, decided that he would fight to save Jews from Nazi horror if he ever had the chance.

2   That chance came in 1940, one year after World War II broke out. By then, the Nazis had conquered France. They ordered French officials to "surrender on demand" any Jew or Nazi enemy. Such people were to be turned over to the Nazi police, called the Gestapo.

3   At this time, the U.S. was still at peace. It did not join the war until the end of 1941. Still, many Americans wanted to

help those trapped by the Nazis. Some of them formed the Emergency Rescue Committee. Its main goal was to get Jewish artists and writers out of France. The committee needed someone to go to France to oversee this effort. The person would risk arrest, torture, and maybe death. Fry had no training for this kind of rescue work. Nonetheless, he volunteered to go. He later wrote, "...I could not remain idle so long as I had the chance at all of saving even a few of [Nazi Germany's] intended victims."

4   Fry was an unlikely hero. He had never done anything brave in his life. He certainly didn't look heroic. Fry was a thin 32-year-old who suffered from ulcers. He was a bookworm and a bird watcher. "All I [knew] about trying to outsmart the Gestapo," he wrote, "[was] what I'd seen in the movies."

5   Still, in August of 1940, Fry flew to the French port city of Marseilles. He had with him a list of 200 specific people he would try to save. He had exit visas to get each of them out of France. He also had $3,000 wrapped around his legs. Fry had planned on staying for just three weeks. But the rescue effort proved so demanding and the need was so great, he stayed for 13 months. "I stayed because the refugees needed me," he later explained. "But it

took courage, and courage [was] a quality I hadn't previously been sure I possessed."

6   Fry set up his office in a local hotel. By day, he ran a simple—and legal— relief agency. His American Relief Center helped people get food, money, and visas. At night, however, Fry did his real work. With the help of a complex network, he arranged the escape of the 200 people on his list. He also helped nearly 2,000 others flee the Nazis.

7   It was hard to get out of Marseilles in 1940. All exit terminals were watched by the police. With the right papers, some of Fry's "clients" managed to leave by train or boat. Most, however, had to sneak out of France. Often they had to be disguised as farm laborers. They carried their possessions in lunch boxes and climbed a secret escape route over the Pyrénées Mountains and into Spain.

8   Fry not only saved people, but he also saved great works of art. Some of these pieces he smuggled out of the country himself. He once took 12 suitcases by train across the border to Spain. In the suitcases was the original score of Anton Bruckner's Third Symphony.

9   Fry, of course, was putting his life on the line. As a citizen of the neutral United States, he had little to fear if he followed Nazi rules. But he didn't follow them.

Night after night he broke the law to aid his refugees. He met with a cartoonist from Vienna who agreed to forge I.D. cards. He raised money on the black market. He kept a map of his secret escape

Varian Fry (seated) with artist Andre Breton in Marseilles, France, 1940

routes pinned to the wall behind a mirror in his hotel room.

10   The police suspected Varian Fry was up to something. They watched him closely. A few times they even brought him in for questioning. So Fry had to be careful. He masked conversations he had in his hotel room by running water in the sink. He got rid of secret papers by burning them in train station bathrooms. He even stuffed secret messages into hollowed-out toothpaste tubes.

11   At last, in September 1941, Varian Fry was ordered out of France. He was labeled an "undesirable alien." When he asked the police why they were kicking him out, one of them said, "Because you have protected Jews and anti-Nazis."

12   Back in the United States, Fry tried to alert U.S. officials to the plight of the Jews under the Nazis. But few people listened to him. Miriam Davenport, who worked with Fry in France, explained why. She said, "We were still pretty anti-Semitic in this country at that time. A lot of people just didn't want to hear his story."

13   Varian Fry died in 1967. At the time he was teaching Latin at a school in Connecticut. Shortly before he died, the French gave him a Legion of Honor award. Later, in 1991, the U.S. honored him with the Eisenhower Liberation Medal. But his greatest tribute came from the Jews themselves. Israel named him "Righteous Among the Nations." This award is given to non-Jews who risked their lives to save Jews. Varian Fry was the first American to win it. As Susan Goodman, the curator of the Jewish Museum in New York, said, "His story shows any person can be a hero." 🍃

If you have been timed while reading this article, enter your reading time below. Then turn to the Words-per-Minute Table on page 71 and look up your reading speed (words per minute). Enter your reading speed on the graph on page 72.

Reading Time: Lesson 7

3 : 52

Minutes   Seconds

A | Finding the Main Idea

One statement below expresses the main idea of the article. One statement is too general, or too broad. The other statement explains only part of the article; it is too narrow. Label the statements using the following key:

M—Main Idea   **B—Too Broad**   **N—Too Narrow**

_N_ 1. Varian Fry once smuggled 12 suitcases of fine art out of France into Spain.

_B_ 2. The injustices done to Jewish citizens by the Nazis outraged people around the world.

_M_ 3. Varian Fry rescued about 2,000 people, many of them Jewish artists and writers, from the Nazis and was much later recognized as a hero for his efforts.

_____ Score 15 points for a correct M answer.

_____ Score 5 points for each correct B or N answer.

_____ **Total Score:** Finding the Main Idea

B | Recalling Facts

How well do you remember the facts in the article? Put an X in the box next to the answer that correctly completes each statement about the article.

1. Before he began his rescue efforts, Varian Fry was a
   ☒ a. writer in New York City.
   ☐ b. famous French artist.
   ☐ c. politician.

2. The main goal of the Emergency Rescue Committee was to
   ☒ a. work toward the downfall of the Nazis.
   ☐ b. smuggle fine art out of France.
   ☒ c. get Jewish artists and writers out of France.

3. Varian Fry did most of his work in the city of
   ☐ a. Paris, France.
   ☒ b. Marseilles, France.
   ☐ c. Berlin, Germany.

4. Varian Fry was ordered out of France in
   ☐ a. January 1939.
   ☒ b. September 1941.
   ☐ c. September 1935.

5. The award Fry received from Israel was the
   ☒ a. "Righteous Among the Nations" award.
   ☐ b. Eisenhower Liberation medal.
   ☐ c. Legion of Honor award.

Score 5 points for each correct answer.

_____ **Total Score:** Recalling Facts

C Making Inferences

When you combine your own experience and information from a text to draw a conclusion that is not directly stated in that text, you are making an inference. Below are five statements that may or may not be inferences based on information in the article. Label the statements using the following key:

C—Correct Inference   F—Faulty Inference

___F___ 1. If Varian Fry hadn't traveled to Germany during the 1930s, he might never have become involved in rescuing Jews from the Nazis.

___C___ 2. Although a nation may remain neutral, that doesn't mean that all of its citizens are also neutral.

___F___ 3. The German police had positive evidence that Varian Fry was helping Jews out of France.

___C___ 4. U.S. Government officials were secretly directing Varian Fry's activities in France.

___C___ 5. Fry himself was surprised at how well he coped with the dangers he faced.

Score 5 points for each correct answer.

_____ **Total Score:** Making Inferences

D Using Words Precisely

Each numbered sentence below contains an underlined word or phrase from the article. Following the sentence are three definitions. One definition is closest to the meaning of the underlined word. One definition is opposite or nearly opposite. Label those two definitions using the following key. Do not label the remaining definition.

C—Closest   O—Opposite or Nearly Opposite

1. Now they had begun a brutal campaign of <u>persecuting</u> the Jews.

   _____ a. identifying

   ___C___ b. tormenting

   ___O___ c. treating with kindness and respect

2. But the rescue effort proved so <u>demanding</u> and the need was so great, he stayed for 13 months.

   ___O___ a. easy

   _____ b. interesting

   ___C___ c. challenging

3. As a citizen of the <u>neutral</u> United States, he had little to fear if he followed Nazi rules.

   ___O___ a. backing one side in a struggle

   ___C___ b. not supporting either side in a struggle

   _____ c. peace-loving

4. He <u>masked</u> conversations he had in his hotel room by running water in the sink.

   ___O___ a. drew attention to

   _____ b. ridiculed

   ___C___ c. covered up

5. She said, "We were still pretty <u>anti-Semitic</u> in this country at that time."

_____ a. against Jews

_____ b. supportive of Jews

_____ c. unaware of Jews

_____ Score 3 points for each correct C answer.

_____ Score 2 points for each correct O answer.

_____ **Total Score:** Using Words Precisely

Enter the four total scores in the spaces below, and add them together to find your Reading Comprehension Score. Then record your score on the graph on page 73.

Score	Question Type	Lesson 7
_____	Finding the Main Idea	
_____	Recalling Facts	
_____	Making Inferences	
_____	Using Words Precisely	
_____	**Reading Comprehension Score**	

Author's Approach

Put an X in the box next to the correct answer.

1. What does the author mean by the statement "They [the Nazis] ordered French officials to 'surrender on demand' any Jew or Nazi enemy"?

☐ a. The French and the Nazis had a friendly, cooperative relationship.

☒ b. The Nazis considered Jews to be dangerous and undesirable.

☐ c. French officials were given the right to make their own decisions about whether or not to follow Nazi rules.

2. The main purpose of the first paragraph is to

☐ a. describe travel during the 1930s.

☐ b. inform the reader about how the U.S. entered World War II.

☒ c. explain the reasons for Varian Fry's later actions.

3. Judging by statements from the article "Saving Jews from the Nazis," you can conclude that the author wants the reader to think that

☒ a. Varian Fry was constantly in danger during his mission.

☒ b. what Varian Fry did demanded a great deal of courage.

☐ c. the United States was solidly behind Varian Fry's efforts.

_____ Number of correct answers

Record your personal assessment of your work on the Critical Thinking Chart on page 74.

Summarizing and Paraphrasing

Put an X in the box next to the correct answer for question 1. Follow the directions provided for question 2.

1. Below are summaries of the article. Choose the summary that says all the most important things about the article but in the fewest words.

☐ a. Varian Fry, outraged at the unfair and brutal treatment of Jews by the Nazis, voluntarily traveled to France to help Jews escape the Nazis. In Marseilles, France, he set up an organization that allowed first artists and writers to escape and then allowed about 2,000 others to flee the Nazis. Although Nazi officials suspected Fry of breaking their laws, they could not prove that he was working against them. Even so, they threw him out of the country in 1941, saying that he had "protected Jews and anti-Nazis."

☐ b. Varian Fry worked hard to save Jews from the Nazis in the years just before the U.S. entered World War II.

☒ c. Varian Fry helped Jews escape the Nazis in France by supplying them with money and the papers needed to get out. Although the Nazis suspected Fry, they were unable to prove his guilt, and so they threw him out of France. Fry later was recognized for his heroism by France, the U.S., and Israel.

2. Reread paragraph 8 in the article. Below, write a summary of the paragraph in no more than 25 words.

He saved art too.

Reread your summary and decide whether it covers the important ideas in the paragraph. Next, decide how to shorten the summary to 15 words or less without leaving out any essential information. Write this summary below.

_____

_____

_____ Number of correct answers

Record your personal assessment of your work on the Critical Thinking Chart on page 74.

Critical Thinking

Put an X in the box next to the correct answer for questions 1, 4, and 5. Follow the directions provided for the other questions.

1. Which of the following statements from the article is an opinion rather than a fact?

☐ a. "Still, in August of 1940, Fry flew to the French port city of Marseilles."

☒ b. "He [Fry] certainly didn't look heroic."

☐ c. "His American Relief Center helped people get food, money, and visas."

2. Choose from the letters below to correctly complete the following statement. Write the letters on the lines.

   In the article, ___*A*___ and ___*C*___ are different in their attitudes toward Jews.

   a. Varian Fry

   b. the Nazis

   c. Miriam Davenport

3. Choose from the letters below to correctly complete the following statement. Write the letters on the lines.

   According to the article, ___*C*___ caused Varian Fry to ___*B*___, and the effect was ___*A*___.

   a. he helped Jews escape from France

   b. feel sympathy for the Jews

   c. Nazi cruelty and injustice against Jews

4. How are Varian Fry's activities related to the theme of this book?

   ☐ a. Varian Fry traveled to Germany just before World War II broke out.

   ☐ b. Varian Fry received a number of awards.

   ☐ c. Fry made it possible for thousands of people to escape abuse and, possibly, death.

5. What did you have to do to answer question 2?

   ☐ a. find a contrast (how things are different)

   ☐ b. find a description (how something looks)

   ☐ c. find a fact (something that you can prove is true)

   _____ Number of correct answers

   Record your personal assessment of your work on the Critical Thinking Chart on page 74.

Personal Response

I wonder why

_____

_____

_____

_____

Self-Assessment

Before reading this article, I already knew

_____

_____

_____

_____

_____

CRITICAL THINKING

Compare and Contrast

Think about the articles you have read in Unit One. Pick four articles that described the most exciting rescues. Write the titles of the articles in the first column of the chart below. Use information you learned from the articles to fill in the empty boxes of the chart.

Title	Where did the rescue take place?	Who was rescued?	Who rescued the person (or animal) in trouble?

I would be most likely to tell a friend about this rescue _____ because _____

_____

_____

Words-per-Minute Table

Unit One

Directions: If you were timed while reading an article, refer to the Reading Time you recorded in the box at the end of the article. Use this words-per-minute table to determine your reading speed for that article. Then plot your reading speed on the graph on page 72.

Lesson / No. of Words	Sample 821	1 969	2 917	3 1010	4 983	5 954	6 1302	7 973	Seconds
1:30	547	646	611	673	655	636	868	649	90
1:40	493	581	550	606	590	572	781	584	100
1:50	448	529	500	551	536	520	710	531	110
2:00	411	485	459	505	492	477	651	487	120
2:10	379	447	423	466	454	440	601	449	130
2:20	352	415	393	433	421	409	558	417	140
2:30	328	388	367	404	393	382	521	389	150
2:40	308	363	344	379	369	358	488	365	160
2:50	290	342	324	356	347	337	460	343	170
3:00	274	323	306	337	328	318	434	324	180
3:10	259	306	290	319	310	301	411	307	190
3:20	246	291	275	303	295	286	391	292	200
3:30	235	277	262	289	281	273	372	278	210
3:40	224	264	250	275	268	260	355	265	220
3:50	214	253	239	263	256	249	340	254	230
4:00	205	242	229	253	246	239	326	243	240
4:10	197	233	220	242	236	229	312	234	250
4:20	189	224	212	233	227	220	300	225	260
4:30	182	215	204	224	218	212	289	216	270
4:40	176	208	197	216	211	204	279	209	280
4:50	170	200	190	209	203	197	269	201	290
5:00	164	194	183	202	197	191	260	195	300
5:10	159	188	177	195	190	185	252	188	310
5:20	154	182	172	189	184	179	244	182	320
5:30	149	176	167	184	179	173	237	177	330
5:40	145	171	162	178	173	168	230	172	340
5:50	141	166	157	173	169	164	223	167	350
6:00	137	162	153	168	164	159	217	162	360
6:10	133	157	149	164	159	155	211	158	370
6:20	130	153	145	159	155	151	206	154	380
6:30	126	149	141	155	151	147	200	150	390
6:40	123	145	138	152	147	143	195	146	400
6:50	120	142	134	148	144	140	191	142	410
7:00	117	138	131	144	140	136	186	139	420
7:10	115	135	128	141	137	133	182	136	430
7:20	112	132	125	138	134	130	178	133	440
7:30	109	129	122	135	131	127	174	130	450
7:40	107	126	120	132	128	124	170	127	460
7:50	105	124	117	129	125	122	166	124	470
8:00	103	121	115	126	123	119	163	122	480

Minutes and Seconds

Plotting Your Progress: Reading Speed

Unit One

Directions: If you were timed while reading an article, write your words-per-minute rate for that article in the box under the number of the lesson. Then plot your reading speed on the graph by putting a small X on the line directly above the number of the lesson, across from the number of words per minute you read. As you mark your speed for each lesson, graph your progress by drawing a line to connect the X's.

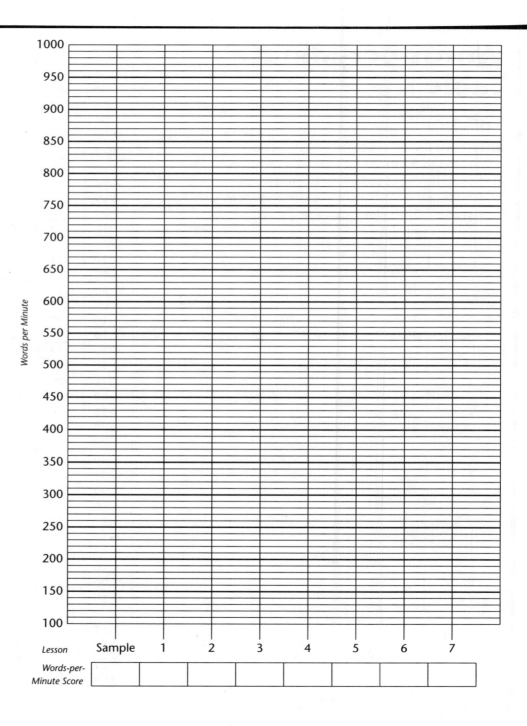

Lesson	Sample	1	2	3	4	5	6	7
Words-per-Minute Score								

Plotting Your Progress: Reading Comprehension

Unit One

Directions: Write your Reading Comprehension score for each lesson in the box under the number of the lesson. Then plot your score on the graph by putting a small X on the line directly above the number of the lesson and across from the score you earned. As you mark your score for each lesson, graph your progress by drawing a line to connect the X's.

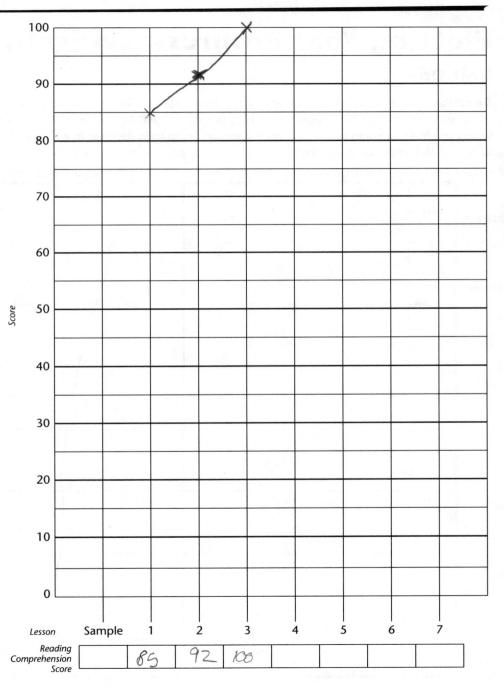

Lesson	Sample	1	2	3	4	5	6	7
Reading Comprehension Score		85	92	100				

Plotting Your Progress: Critical Thinking

Unit One

Directions: Work with your teacher to evaluate your responses to the Critical Thinking questions for each lesson. Then fill in the appropriate spaces in the chart below. For each lesson and each type of Critical Thinking question, do the following: Mark a minus sign (–) in the box to indicate areas in which you feel you could improve. Mark a plus sign (+) to indicate areas in which you feel you did well. Mark a minus-slash-plus sign (–/+) to indicate areas in which you had mixed success. Then write any comments you have about your performance, including ideas for improvement.

Lesson	Author's Approach	Summarizing and Paraphrasing	Critical Thinking
Sample			
1			
2			
3			
4			
5			
6			
7			

UNIT TWO

LOVE WORKS A MIRACLE

There goes Cruiser again," thought Cindy Dunlop when she heard a splash in the family swimming pool. Cruiser, a springer spaniel, frequently jumped into the pool just for fun. Cindy was in the garage around the corner from the patio. She was talking on the phone to a friend who had called to chat.

2   But suddenly Cindy sensed that something was wrong. The splash she had heard was followed by dead silence. Quickly Cindy said goodbye and hung up the phone. She hurried around the corner and saw—to her horror—her 17-month-old daughter, Kyla, floating face down in the 15 × 30-foot pool. Cruiser was running back and forth along the edge of the pool, trying to save the child by grabbing Kyla's clothing with his teeth.

3   Most mothers would have simply jumped into the pool and pulled their child to safety. But Cindy Dunlop was not like most mothers. She was paralyzed from the chest down as a result of an automobile crash 12 years before. It had left her with two broken shoulder blades,

Cindy Dunlop holds her 17-month-old daughter Kyla after rescuing the child from the family swimming pool. Cruiser, the family dog, tried to save Kyla by grabbing her clothes with his teeth.

a broken back, and a severed spinal cord. Because of her disability, Cindy had been forced to adjust to life in a wheelchair. At 90 pounds, Cindy swam regularly for physical therapy but needed assistance getting in and out of the pool.

4   Now, on October 7, 1986, Kyla's life rested in her mother's hands. Cindy didn't have time to phone for help. There wasn't anyone nearby, anyway. The Dunlops lived in the isolated desert town of El Mirage, California. Cindy's husband, Ron, had gone off to work several hours earlier. The nearest rescue squad was 25 miles away. And the nearest neighbor was half a mile down the road.

5   Knowing she couldn't grab Kyla from the edge of the pool, Cindy had only one choice. She drove her wheelchair straight into the chilly water. As the chair sank, Cindy began to swim over to Kyla, who was still floating, face down, 25 feet away.

Because of the warm climate, many homes in California have backyard swimming pools.

When Cindy reached her daughter, she managed to flip her over. Then she grabbed her and towed her to the edge of the pool. Kyla's eyes were closed and her lips were blue. She wasn't breathing.

6   Frantic with fear and panic, Cindy tried to lift Kyla up and out of the water while holding onto the edge of the pool with one arm. "She was so limp and heavy, I couldn't," she later said.

7   Cindy realized she would have to find another way to get Kyla out. She took a deep breath and let herself sink to the bottom of the pool. With her arms under Kyla's body and her fingertips gripping the edge of the pool, Cindy used her head to push the child upward. She managed to lift Kyla out of the water, but couldn't get her over the edge onto the concrete. When she tried, the little girl fell backward into the pool.

8   Desperately, Cindy kept trying. Finally, by keeping her head straighter, she was able to roll Kyla up and out of the water. Then, propping herself up on her elbows at the edge of the pool, Cindy reached out and turned Kyla toward her. Her daughter still wasn't breathing. With fear gripping her heart, Cindy pinched the child's nose

shut and began puffing short breaths into her mouth.

9   At first, there was no response. Again and again Cindy puffed breaths into Kyla's mouth. Finally, Kyla's body lurched, and she began to cough and spit up water. Then the little girl started to cry. "It was the greatest thing in the world to hear that scream," Cindy said.

10   The crisis wasn't over yet. Cindy still needed to get to a telephone—fast—in order to dial 911. She had no way of knowing if Kyla might be suffering brain damage from lack of oxygen. In addition, the little girl could go into shock at any moment. But how was Cindy going to get out of the pool without assistance? By habit, she swam to the other side, where her husband always helped her out. Then, using every bit of strength she had left, Cindy pulled her upper torso over the edge. She reached down and lifted her legs up. Only then did she realize she had left Kyla alone at the other edge of the pool. What if the little girl fell back in? Grimly, Cindy crawled on her belly across the concrete rim to the other side.

11   Cindy lifted Kyla onto her stomach. She wriggled on her back to the middle of

the lawn. Then, with Kyla safely away from the pool, Cindy made her way to the only phone she could reach without her wheelchair. It was in the bedroom. "[I] crawled Army style with just my arms into the bedroom," she later remembered.

12   Cindy called 911, and she and Kyla were rushed to St. Mary's Desert Valley Hospital. Cindy's feet, elbows, and hands were badly scraped from crawling across the concrete. Kyla, however, was fine. Before long, she was giggling and playing as if nothing had happened.

If you have been timed while reading this article, enter your reading time below. Then turn to the Words-per-Minute Table on page 133 and look up your reading speed (words per minute). Enter your reading speed on the graph on page 134.

Reading Time: Lesson 8

_____5___ : ___00___
Minutes   Seconds

A | Finding the Main Idea

One statement below expresses the main idea of the article. One statement is too general, or too broad. The other statement explains only part of the article; it is too narrow. Label the statements using the following key:

M—Main Idea   **B—Too Broad**   **N—Too Narrow**

___B___ 1. Backyard pools may pose a danger to young children who are left unsupervised, even if only for a few minutes.

___N___ 2. Cindy Dunlop had been paralyzed from the chest down in an automobile crash.

___M___ 3. Although she was confined to a wheelchair, Cindy Dunlop managed to save her daughter from drowning in the family pool.

_____ Score 15 points for a correct M answer.

_____ Score 5 points for each correct B or N answer.

_____ **Total Score:** Finding the Main Idea

B | Recalling Facts

How well do you remember the facts in the article? Put an X in the box next to the answer that correctly completes each statement about the article.

1. When Cindy first heard a splash, she thought that
   - ☐ a. a neighbor had stopped over for a quick swim.
   - ☐ b. Kyla, her daughter, had fallen into the pool.
   - ☒ c. her dog, Cruiser, had jumped in for a swim.

2. Although Cindy Dunlop had regular physical therapy in the pool, she
   - ☐ a. disliked swimming.
   - ☒ b. needed help getting in and out of the pool.
   - ☐ c. had never learned how to swim by herself.

3. Cindy finally got Kyla out of the pool by
   - ☐ a. calling 911.
   - ☒ b. keeping her head straight and pushing hard.
   - ☐ c. having her dog, Cruiser, pull Kyla out.

4. Just after Kyla came out of the water, Cindy Dunlop
   - ☒ a. puffed breaths into Kyla's mouth.
   - ☐ b. called 911.
   - ☐ c. lifted Kyla onto her stomach.

5. As a result of the accident, Kyla
   - ☒ a. suffered no major physical damage.
   - ☐ b. suffered brain damage.
   - ☐ c. went into deep shock.

_____ Score 5 points for each correct answer.

_____ **Total Score:** Recalling Facts

C Making Inferences

When you combine your own experience and information from a text to draw a conclusion that is not directly stated in that text, you are making an inference. Below are five statements that may or may not be inferences based on information in the article. Label the statements using the following key:

C—Correct Inference   **F—Faulty Inference**

___C___ 1. Cruiser was aware that Kyla was in trouble.

___F___ 2. Kyla was an exceptionally large and heavy child for her age.

___C___ 3. Cindy Dunlop was familiar with basic lifesaving techniques.

___C___ 4. Cindy Dunlop's quick thinking saved Kyla's life.

___F___ 5. Cindy Dunlop paid no attention to the fact that she was scraping her feet, elbows, and hands by crawling on the cement.

Score 5 points for each correct answer.

_____ **Total Score:** Making Inferences

D Using Words Precisely

Each numbered sentence below contains an underlined word or phrase from the article. Following the sentence are three definitions. One definition is closest to the meaning of the underlined word. One definition is opposite or nearly opposite. Label those two definitions using the following key. Do not label the remaining definition.

C—Closest   **O—Opposite or Nearly Opposite**

1. Cruiser, a springer spaniel, <u>frequently</u> jumped into the pool just for fun.

   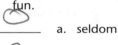 a. seldom

   ___C___ b. often

   _____ c. disobediently

2. She hurried around the corner and saw—to her <u>horror</u>—her 17-month-old daughter, Kyla, floating face down in the 15 x 30-foot pool.

   _____ a. surprise

   ___O___ b. delight

   ___C___ c. extreme terror

3. It [the accident] had left her with two broken shoulder blades, a broken back, and a <u>severed</u> spinal cord.

   ___C___ a. cut into two

   _____ b. painful

   ___O___ c. whole

4. The Dunlops lived in the isolated desert town of El Mirage, California.

_____ a. close-to-everything

_____ b. out-of-the-way

_____ c. famous

5. Finally, Kyla's body lurched, and she began to cough and spit up water.

_____ a. jerked

_____ b. became cold

_____ c. moved slowly and gracefully

_____ Score 3 points for each correct C answer.

_____ Score 2 points for each correct O answer.

_____ **Total Score:** Using Words Precisely

Enter the four total scores in the spaces below, and add them together to find your Reading Comprehension Score. Then record your score on the graph on page 135.

Score	Question Type	Lesson 8
_____	Finding the Main Idea	
_____	Recalling Facts	
_____	Making Inferences	
_____	Using Words Precisely	
_____	**Reading Comprehension Score**	

Author's Approach

Put an X in the box next to the correct answer.

1. What does the author mean by the statement "Now, on October 7, 1986, Kyla's life rested in her mother's hands"?

☐ a. That day, Kyla felt the comfort of her mother's hands.

☐ b. If Kyla's mother's hands were strong enough, Kyla would live; if they weren't, she would die.

☒ c. The decisions and actions of her mother that day would mean life or death to Kyla.

2. The author probably wrote this article in order to

☐ a. persuade people not to have backyard swimming pools.

☒ b. tell the story of a courageous woman who rescued her daughter.

☐ c. create a loving mood.

3. The author tells this story mainly by

☒ a. telling about events in the order they happened.

☐ b. comparing different topics.

☐ c. telling different stories about the same topic.

_____ Number of correct answers

Record your personal assessment of your work on the Critical Thinking Chart on page 136.

CRITICAL THINKING

Summarizing and Paraphrasing

Follow the directions provided for question 1. Put an X in the box next to the correct answer for question 2.

1. Look for the important ideas and events in paragraphs 5 and 6. Summarize those paragraphs in one or two sentences.

   Wheelchair & all, Cindy went into the water to rescue her child, but she had difficulty.

2. Read the statement about the article below. Then read the paraphrase of that statement. Choose the reason that best tells why the paraphrase does not say the same thing as the statement.

   Statement: The Dunlops lived in an isolated area, Cindy's husband had gone to work, and the nearest neighbor was a half mile down the road.

   Paraphrase: Cindy was sometimes nervous during the day because she lived in an isolated area, her husband went to work, and it was about a half a mile to the nearest neighbor.

   ☒ a. Paraphrase says too much.

   ☐ b. Paraphrase doesn't say enough.

   ☐ c. Paraphrase doesn't agree with the statement about the article.

   _____ Number of correct answers

   Record your personal assessment of your work on the Critical Thinking Chart on page 136.

Critical Thinking

Put an X in the box next to the correct answer for questions 1, 2, 4, and 5. Follow the directions provided for question 3.

1. Which of the following statements from the article is an opinion rather than a fact?

   ☐ a. "She [Cindy Dunlop] was paralyzed from the chest down as a result of an automobile crash 12 years before."

   ☐ b. "The Dunlops lived in the isolated desert town of El Mirage, California."

   ☒ c. "It was the greatest thing in the world to hear that scream."

2. From the article, you can predict that if Cindy Dunlop hadn't heard the splash of her daughter falling into the pool,

   ☐ a. Cruiser would have rescued Kyla by himself.

   ☒ b. Kyla might have drowned.

   ☒ c. She would probably have sensed that Kyla was in trouble anyway.

3. Choose from the letters below to correctly complete the following statement. Write the letters on the lines.

   On the positive side, ____C____, but on the negative side ____A____.

   a. Both Cindy and Kyla Dunlop were badly frightened by the experience.

   b. Both Cindy and Kyla were treated at the same hospital.

   c. Cindy Dunlop was able to save her daughter from drowning.

4. What was the cause of Cindy Dunlop's scraped feet, elbows, and hands?

   ☐ a. Cindy drove her wheelchair into the pool.

   ☐ b. Cindy rolled Kyla up and out of the water.

   ☒ c. Cindy had crawled across concrete.

CRITICAL THINKING

5. If you were taking care of a child near a pool, how could you use the information in the article to keep him or her safe?

    a. Keep your eye on the child at all times.

    b. Leave a trustworthy dog in charge if you have to leave the child alone.

    ☐ c. If you get called away to answer the phone, limit your conversation to 10 or 15 minutes in length.

_____ Number of correct answers

Record your personal assessment of your work on the Critical Thinking Chart on page 136.

Self-Assessment

I can't really understand how

_____

_____

_____

_____

Personal Response

Describe a time when you were supposed to care for a younger child and something frightening or unexpected happened.

_____

_____

_____

_____

DRAMA ON THE HIGH SEAS

It was an enticing promise. Take a cruise aboard "the fun ship" to "exotic, glamorous Nassau." Indeed, the *Yarmouth Castle* had all the trappings of a party ship—balloons, music, dancing, and lots of food and drinks. Twice a week it made an overnight cruise from Miami, Florida, to Nassau in the Bahamas. But the cruise that began at 5 P.M. on December 12, 1965, turned out to be anything but fun.

2   All the glitter seen on the *Yarmouth Castle* covered up one grim fact—the ship was a floating fire trap. The 5,000-ton vessel was 38 years old. Most modern ships of that size are built using little or no wood. But this one had tons of inflammable paneling and furniture. Also, although the ship used Miami—an American city—as its port, it sailed under the flag of Panama. For that reason, it was considered a foreign ship. It didn't have to meet the strict safety standards set by the United States for its own ships. Rules were so lax on the *Yarmouth Castle* that on many trips no one bothered to hold a lifeboat drill. Worse, no one bothered to tell passengers where they could find life jackets in case of an emergency.

Fire sweeps through the cruise ship Yarmouth Castle *in the Atlantic Ocean, 120 miles east of Miami. Inset photo: the* U.S.S. Constitution *is a cruise ship similar to the* Yarmouth Castle.

3   When the *Yarmouth Castle* set sail that December evening, there were 376 passengers and a crew of 176 on board. One crew member was a 23-year-old Canadian named Terry Wise. Wise, an assistant purser, was delighted just to be on the ship. This was his first-ever job at sea. He had only started working on the *Yarmouth Castle* two days earlier.

4   Things went smoothly at first. The passengers began eating, drinking, and dancing the night away. By 1:30 A.M., the *Yarmouth Castle* was about 135 miles east of Miami. Only the party diehards were still up. Everyone else had gone to bed. Suddenly, a fellow crew member pounded on Terry Wise's cabin door. "Wake up!" he said, "There's smoke out here!"

5   Wise jumped out of bed and put on his white uniform. Maybe, he thought, someone had tossed a cigarette into a wastebasket. But when Wise opened his door, he saw the corridor was black with smoke. He ran back inside and wrapped a thick, wet towel around his face. Crouching low, he went back out into the corridor. Groping his way in the dark, he began banging on cabin doors to wake people up. Then, after crawling up the several sets of stairs, he emerged on the stern of the ship's deck.

6   As Wise looked at the ship, he couldn't believe his eyes. The whole front of the vessel was ablaze. Strong winds were fanning the flames. Panicky people, some half naked, ran about, shouting for their loved ones. Others lay on the deck crying. Still others never got out of their rooms.

7   Lloyd Lamn, a volunteer fire fighter, was on the cruise. He later said, "It was the worst fire I've ever seen—a roaring inferno from the bottom to the top."

8   Most crew members had no clue what to do. They appeared to be just as confused as the passengers. The fire spread

Terry Wise (shown here with his daughter) was responsible for saving over 30 passengers from the fire on the Yarmouth Castle.

to the bridge so quickly that no distress signal was sent. By the time the captain had gotten out of bed, the fire was out of control. Meanwhile, Wise tried to figure out what he could do to save people. With two other members of the crew, he grabbed a fire hose. But when they turned it on, there was no water.

9 All the lifeboats near the bow were on fire. But the fire had not yet spread to the stern. Desperately, Wise and a few others in the stern tried to swing a lifeboat over the railing. As they did, Wise saw some crew members fighting with passengers over who was going to get on board. Wise hollered, "Women and children first!"— but no one listened. Then Wise saw the captain and several other people rowing away in a lifeboat.

10 Arnold Goldman, along with his wife and two children, made it up to the top deck. The family scrambled onto a lifeboat and waited to be lowered. But all at once, the boat shifted and dropped at an odd angle. It looked as if it might break away from the ship altogether and plunge six stories into the sea. If the Goldmans fell that far, they might well die. They were dangling too far below the ship to simply step back on board, but Goldman managed to swing his two children back up and over the railing. He couldn't lift his wife back onto the ship, however. "Someone help us!" he shouted.

11 Terry Wise rushed to the rescue. Goldman lifted his wife into Wise's arms and then clambered back on board himself. After rescuing Mrs. Goldman, Wise began throwing everything that would float down to the people in the water who had no life jackets.

12 Luckily, other ships were in the vicinity. The captains of the *Bahama Star* and the *Finnpulp* saw the fire and set a course straight for the stricken ship. Once they got close enough, they lowered their lifeboats and pulled many people out of the sea.

13 Back on the *Yarmouth Castle*, Wise accompanied Goldman and his family to a lower deck, then told them to jump into the water so they could be picked up. Wise even gave his own life jacket to Goldman, who had none. As the Goldmans prepared to jump, Wise looked for others in trouble. He dragged dozens of people away from the fire. He found one woman so badly burned that there were only a few strands of hair left on her head. Wise wrapped her in wet rags and helped her get to a lifeboat. Others, mostly elderly, were frozen in fear; they refused to move. Wise had to pry their fingers from the railing. Then, checking to make sure their life jackets were secure, he lifted them one by one over the railing and dropped them into the water, where they were quickly picked up and brought to safety.

14 Captain Carl Brown of the *Bahama Star* could see that there was only one officer left on the *Yarmouth Castle*. It was Wise. All the others had abandoned ship. "That man," said Brown, "[saved] a lot of lives."

15 At last, Wise heard a shout from the *Bahama Star*, "Jump—there's no one else left!" It was true. Wise was the only living person left on the *Yarmouth Castle*. And so at last he climbed over the railing and shimmied down a rope to a waiting lifeboat. In all, he had saved over 30 lives. But 88 passengers and two crew members had died in the inferno. When the *Yarmouth Castle* finally sank beneath the waves, it took those 90 bodies with it.

If you have been timed while reading this article, enter your reading time below. Then turn to the Words-per-Minute Table on page 133 and look up your reading speed (words per minute). Enter your reading speed on the graph on page 134.

Reading Time: Lesson 9

_____ : _____
Minutes   Seconds

A | Finding the Main Idea

One statement below expresses the main idea of the article. One statement is too general, or too broad. The other statement explains only part of the article; it is too narrow. Label the statements using the following key:

M—Main Idea   **B—Too Broad**   **N—Too Narrow**

 1. A total of 90 people died when the poorly-run cruise ship *Yarmouth Castle* caught fire at sea, however a brave crew member was able to save over 30 lives.

 2. Two ships, the *Bahama Star* and *Finnpulp* came to the rescue of the passengers of *Yarmouth Castle*.

_____ 3. A fire aboard a ship at sea can be extremely dangerous.

_____ Score 15 points for a correct M answer.

_____ Score 5 points for each correct B or N answer.

_____ **Total Score:** Finding the Main Idea

B | Recalling Facts

How well do you remember the facts in the article? Put an X in the box next to the answer that correctly completes each statement about the article.

1. The *Yarmouth Castle* was headed from Miami to
☒ a. Nassau in the Bahamas.
☐ b. Cuba.
☐ c. Key West, Florida.

2. Unlike most modern ships, the *Yarmouth Castle*
☒ a. sailed under the Panama flag.
☐ b. had plenty of inflammable paneling and furniture.
☐ c. started its trip from Miami, Florida.

3. After the fire started, most crew members
☐ a. did everything they could to help the passengers.
☐ b. followed the written rules perfectly.
☒ c. didn't know what to do.

4. The captain of the *Yarmouth Castle*
☐ a. quickly wired other ships for help.
☒ b. abandoned ship before most of his passengers could.
☐ c. fought the fire himself.

5. The last living person on board was
☐ a. the captain.
☐ b. Arnold Goldman.
☒ c. the assistant purser, Terry Wise.

_____ Score 5 points for each correct answer.

_____ **Total Score:** Recalling Facts

C | Making Inferences

When you combine your own experience and information from a text to draw a conclusion that is not directly stated in that text, you are making an inference. Below are five statements that may or may not be inferences based on information in the article. Label the statements using the following key:

C—Correct Inference   F—Faulty Inference

_C_   1. If the *Yarmouth Castle* had flown the U.S. flag, it would most likely have been safer.

_C_   2. On ships that are allowed fly the U.S. flag, lifeboat drills must be held regularly.

_F_   3. The captain of the *Yarmouth Castle* instilled a sense of duty and pride in his crew.

_C_   4. Many passengers and their families were grateful to Terry Wise.

_C_   5. Several officers from nearby ships joined Terry Wise on board the *Yarmouth Castle* and helped him lift passengers onto lifeboats.

Score 5 points for each correct answer.

_____ **Total Score:** Making Inferences

D | Using Words Precisely

Each numbered sentence below contains an underlined word or phrase from the article. Following the sentence are three definitions. One definition is closest to the meaning of the underlined word. One definition is opposite or nearly opposite. Label those two definitions using the following key. Do not label the remaining definition.

C—Closest   O—Opposite or Nearly Opposite

1. It was an <u>enticing</u> promise.

_C_   a. distasteful

_____   b. old-fashioned

_O_   c. attractive

2. But this one had tons of <u>inflammable</u> paneling and furniture.

_C_   a. ready to burn

_____   b. wood

_O_   c. impossible to burn

3. Rules were so <u>lax</u> on the *Yarmouth Castle* that on some trips no one bothered to hold a lifeboat drill.

_____   a. easily misunderstood

_C_   b. slack or careless

_O_   c. rigid and precise

4. "It was the worst fire I've ever seen—a roaring <u>inferno</u> from the bottom to the top."

_C_   a. huge fire

_O_   b. cold spot

_____   c. major accident

5. The captains...saw the fire and set a course straight for the <u>stricken</u> ship.

_____ a. overcrowded

___C___ b. injured

___O___ c. perfect

_____ Score 3 points for each correct C answer.

_____ Score 2 points for each correct O answer.

_____ **Total Score:** Using Words Precisely

Enter the four total scores in the spaces below, and add them together to find your Reading Comprehension Score. Then record your score on the graph on page 135.

Score	Question Type	Lesson 9
_____	Finding the Main Idea	
_____	Recalling Facts	
_____	Making Inferences	
_____	Using Words Precisely	
_____	**Reading Comprehension Score**	

Author's Approach

Put an X in the box next to the correct answer.

1. What is the author's purpose in writing "Drama on the High Seas"?

☐ a. To encourage the reader to go on a cruise

☒ b. To inform the reader about one man who risked his life to save passengers on a cruise

☐ c. To entertain the reader with a romantic story

2. Judging by statements from the article "Drama on the High Seas," you can conclude that the author wants the reader to think that

☒ a. The captain of the *Yarmouth Castle* ignored his duties.

☐ b. Most captains would have abandoned their ships just as the captain of the *Yarmouth Castle* did.

☐ c. The captain of the *Yarmouth Castle* did his best to help his passengers.

3. How is the author's purpose for writing the article expressed in paragraph 14?

☐ a. This paragraph describes the actions of most crew members.

☒ b. In this paragraph, Captain Brown states that Terry Brown saved many lives.

☒ c. This paragraph states that Captain Brown could see aboard the *Yarmouth Castle* from his own ship, the *Bahama Star*.

_____ Number of correct answers

Record your personal assessment of your work on the Critical Thinking Chart on page 136.

Summarizing and Paraphrasing

Put an X in the box next to the correct answer for question 1. Follow the directions provided for the other questions.

1. Below are summaries of the article. Choose the summary that says all the most important things about the article but in the fewest words.

☐ a. The *Yarmouth Castle* caught fire at sea and heavy winds fanned the flames until the boat actually sank.

☒ b. Terry Wise helped people escape the flames on the *Yarmouth Castle* and made sure that people boarding the lifeboats were wearing lifejackets.

☐ c. When the cruise ship *Yarmouth Castle* caught fire at sea, most of the crew abandoned ship, leaving passengers to face the danger alone. Only Terry Wise, a newly-hired crew member tried to rescue the frantic passengers. Despite his efforts, 90 people died.

2. Reread paragraph 15 in the article. Below, write a summary of the paragraph in no more than 25 words.

Wise, saved himself & many others.

Reread your summary and decide whether it covers the important ideas in the paragraph. Next, decide how to shorten the summary to 15 words or less without leaving out any essential information. Write this summary below.

3. Choose the sentence that correctly restates the following sentence from the article:

"The captains of the *Bahama Star* and the *Finnpulp* saw the fire and set a course straight for the stricken ship."

☐ a. The captains of the *Bahama Star* and the *Finnpulp* were unable to stop their ships, and they ran right into the injured ship.

☐ b. The captains of the *Bahama Star* and the *Finnpulp* set the fire and then planned how to intercept the injured ship.

☒ c. After they saw the flames, the captains of the *Bahama Star* and the *Finnpulp* changed their trip plans and sailed toward the ship in trouble.

_____ Number of correct answers

Record your personal assessment of your work on the Critical Thinking Chart on page 136.

Critical Thinking

Put an X in the box next to the correct answer for questions 1, 3, and 4. Follow the directions provided for the other question.

1. Considering the captain of the *Yarmouth Castle*'s actions as described in this article, you can predict that he will be

☐ a. congratulated by other sea captains for escaping unharmed.

☐ b. thanked by the families of the passengers.

☒ c. punished in some way.

2. Choose from the letters below to correctly complete the following statement. Write the letters on the lines.

In the article, _b_ and _b_ are different.

   a.   the fate of the *Yarmouth Castle*

   b.   the fate of the *Bahama Star*

   c.   the fate of the *Finnpulp*

3. What was the effect of the fire aboard the *Yarmouth Castle*?

☐ a.   The ship sailed from Miami, Florida.

☒ b.   A total of 90 people died.

☐ c.   No one bother to have a fire drill on the *Yarmouth Castle*.

4. What did you have to do to answer question 2?

☐ a.   find an opinion (what someone thinks about something)

☒ b.   find a contrast (how things are different)

☐ c.   find a list (a number of things)

+---

_____ Number of correct answers

Record your personal assessment of your work on the Critical Thinking Chart on page 136.

+---

Personal Response

I can't believe

_____

_____

_____

Self-Assessment

One good question about this article that was not asked would be

_____

_____

_____

and the answer is

_____

_____

_____

_____

RESCUE IN PERU

It all began as a party. The Japanese ambassador to Peru hosted a gala event on December 17, 1996. Hundreds of people came to his elegant home in the capital city of Lima, Peru. The guests chatted and mingled with each other. Waiters passed out the champagne. Then, without warning, a blast rocked the rear of the building. Fourteen terrorists waving guns poured into the house. Within seconds, all the guests were lying face down on the floor. The world was in for another long hostage crisis.

2   There were lots of VIPs (very important persons) at the party. Guests included top diplomats from many nations. There were judges and army officers. And there were dozens of rich men and women. The terrorists did not want money, however. They were part of a radical group called Tupac Amaru. (The name came from an 18th century native who led an uprising against the Spanish rulers of Peru.) The rebels, some of whom were teenagers, wanted the release of about 450 of their jailed comrades.

3   Alberto Fujimori, the tough president of Peru, was not about to give in to this demand. He called it "blackmail."

Peruvian special forces storm the Japanese Embassy to free the 72 hostages still held by the Tupac Amaru.

Publicly, Fujimori said he wanted to end the crisis without bloodshed. In secret, however, he ordered the army to plan an assault on the house. He wanted this plan ready to go if negotiations with the terrorists broke down.

4   Over the first few days, the rebels released hundreds of hostages, including all the women. But they kept 72 men. And that was the way things remained until the middle of April. It was a game of cat and mouse. Negotiators met with both sides, but the standoff continued. With patience and hope running out, something had to give.

5   Meanwhile, the Peruvian army had been preparing its secret plans for assault. Several hundred men had gone to a secluded naval base to train. The soldiers used a full-scale plywood mock-up of the ambassador's house. By April, an elite rescue team of 140 men had been put

Peruvian President Fujimori inspects the Japanese Embassy after special forces freed the hostages.

together. "There were only officers, no enlisted men, the best of the best," said one official.

6   While the rescue team trained, other army personnel were digging tunnels under the ambassador's house. To cover the noise of the digging, the army paraded tanks in the streets and played loud music. From the tunnels, the men poked tiny periscopes up into the house. Using the periscopes, they could watch every move the terrorists made.

7   In March the rebels found out about the tunnels and moved to the second floor. But they could not avoid the special plane which flew overhead. Using hi-tech heat-sensing devices, the plane could track the movement of everyone inside the house. Also, the army contacted doctors who were allowed to visit the hostages. The army got these doctors to plant listening "bugs" inside the house. One bug was sewn inside a shirt. Another was placed inside a religious image sent by a wife to her husband. "We knew perfectly the location of terrorists and the majority of the hostages," Fujimori later said. Faced with such a determined foe, the rebels never stood a chance.

8   During this time, the mood inside the ambassador's house was a mixture of boredom and apprehension. It was especially tough on the hostages, many of whom were elderly. "The situation got more tense as time went on," said one negotiator.

"[The hostages] never knew when they went to sleep if they would wake up alive. They were reaching the end of their endurance."

9   The breaking point came when the rebels threatened to cut off medical aid to the hostages. For Fujimori, that was the last straw. The lives of the captives were now in direct jeopardy, and Fujimori was not going to stand for it.

10   April 22 began as another dull day for the terrorists as well as for their hostages. By this time the siege had dragged on for more than four months. In the early afternoon, eight rebels were playing soccer in the massive tile foyer on the first floor. They were dressed in the brightly colored T-shirts of their favorite teams. They used a "ball" they had made from cloth and tape. The remaining terrorists were leaning over a second floor banister, watching the match.

11   Unknown to the rebels, the 140-man rescue team had moved into place. Some crawled into the tunnels beneath the house and the garden. There they planted explosives right under the feet of the soccer-playing rebels. Other commandos crept onto the roof. Their job would be to grab the hostages and get them out of the house safely. A third group was poised to attack through the front door.

12   At last, about half past 3 o'clock, President Fujimori gave the signal to strike. "There was no other way out," he later

said. "I didn't waver for a single minute in giving the order for this rescue operation."

13   The attack was so swift and so well planned that the rebels had no time to respond. A huge explosion ripped through the roof of the foyer, killing or wounding several of the rebels. At the same instant, commandos smashed through the front door and lobbed tear gas through a side window. Using hand grenades and rifles, the soldiers killed all 14 rebels. Before the rebels died, however, they managed to kill two of the soldiers. They also shot one of the hostages, who later died of a heart attack in the hospital. Several other hostages were wounded, but they were all rescued. It took less than 15 minutes for the army to do the job. Then Fujimori announced to the world, "The rebels have been annihilated."

If you have been timed while reading this article, enter your reading time below. Then turn to the Words-per-Minute Table on page 133 and look up your reading speed (words per minute). Enter your reading speed on the graph on page 134.

Reading Time: Lesson 10

_____ : _____
Minutes   Seconds

A Finding the Main Idea

One statement below expresses the main idea of the article. One statement is too general, or too broad. The other statement explains only part of the article; it is too narrow. Label the statements using the following key:

M—Main Idea   **B—Too Broad**   **N—Too Narrow**

____N____ 1. Alberto Fujimori assembled an elite group of officers to fight back against 14 terrorists.

____B____ 2. Many people believe that terrorism should never be tolerated, but should be attacked forcefully.

____M____ 3. The president of Peru responded with force when terrorists held guests captive for months in the home of the Japanese ambassador in Lima, Peru.

_____

_____ Score 15 points for a correct M answer.

_____ Score 5 points for each correct B or N answer.

_____ **Total Score:** Finding the Main Idea

B Recalling Facts

How well do you remember the facts in the article? Put an X in the box next to the answer that correctly completes each statement about the article.

1. The hostage crisis began on
   - ☒ a. December 17, 1996.
   - ☐ b. April 22, 1996.
   - ☐ c. April 22, 1998.

2. The terrorist group wanted
   - ☐ a. a great deal of money in return for the release of the hostages.
   - ☒ b. the release of 450 of their jailed friends.
   - ☐ c. to take over the Peruvian government.

3. To cover up the sound of workers building a tunnel,
   - ☒ a. the army played loud music.
   - ☐ b. helicopters hovered over the house constantly.
   - ☐ c. the army fired on the house day and night.

4. Bugs were set up in the house by
   - ☐ a. terrorists who no longer wished to cooperate with their comrades.
   - ☐ b. soldiers who entered at night.
   - ☒ c. visiting doctors.

5. The attack on the terrorists was over in just under
   - ☐ a. four minutes.
   - ☒ b. 15 minutes.
   - ☐ c. 45 minutes.

_____

Score 5 points for each correct answer.

_____ **Total Score:** Recalling Facts

C | Making Inferences

When you combine your own experience and information from a text to draw a conclusion that is not directly stated in that text, you are making an inference. Below are five statements that may or may not be inferences based on information in the article. Label the statements using the following key:

C—Correct Inference   F—Faulty Inference

_F_ 1. The security at the Japanese ambassador's party was unusually tight.

_F_ 2. Fujimori did not care at all about the safety of the hostages.

_C_ 3. The terrorists had planned their attack on the ambassador's party carefully.

_C_ 4. Negotiators didn't really want the negotiations to work; they secretly wanted to see the terrorists killed.

_F_ 5. The terrorists had received a warning that Fujimori was going to attack on April 22.

Score 5 points for each correct answer.

_____ **Total Score:** Making Inferences

D | Using Words Precisely

Each numbered sentence below contains an underlined word or phrase from the article. Following the sentence are three definitions. One definition is closest to the meaning of the underlined word. One definition is opposite or nearly opposite. Label those two definitions using the following key. Do not label the remaining definition.

C—Closest   O—Opposite or Nearly Opposite

1. Several hundred men had gone to a <u>secluded</u> naval base to train.

_O_ a. busy and well-known

_C_ b. lonely and hidden

_____ c. well-equipped

2. By April, an <u>elite</u> rescue team of 140 men had been put together.

_O_ a. inferior

_____ b. illegal

_C_ c. superior

3. Faced with such a determined <u>foe</u>, the rebels never stood a chance.

_O_ a. friend

_C_ b. enemy

_____ c. force

4. The lives of the captives were now in direct <u>jeopardy</u>, and Fujimori was not going to stand for it.

_C_ a. danger

_O_ b. safety

_____ c. pathway

5. Then Fujimori announced to the world, "The rebels have been <u>annihilated</u>."

_____ a. outsmarted

_____ b. given aid

_____ c. destroyed completely

_____ Score 3 points for each correct C answer.

_____ Score 2 points for each correct O answer.

_____ **Total Score:** Using Words Precisely

Enter the four total scores in the spaces below, and add them together to find your Reading Comprehension Score. Then record your score on the graph on page 135.

Score	Question Type	Lesson 10
_____	Finding the Main Idea	
_____	Recalling Facts	
_____	Making Inferences	
_____	Using Words Precisely	
_____	**Reading Comprehension Score**	

Author's Approach

Put an X in the box next to the correct answer.

1. What is the author's purpose in writing "Rescue in Peru"?

☐ a. To express an opinion about terrorism

☐ b. To inform the reader about the demands of rebel forces in Peru

☒ c. To describe a situation in which many people were rescued from terrorists

2. Which of the following statements from the article best describes Alberto Fujimori's thoughts after terrorists threatened to cut off medical aid to the hostages?

☐ a. "Then Fujimori announced to the world, 'The rebels have been annihilated.'"

☐ b. "Publicly, Fujimori said he wanted to end the crisis without bloodshed."

☒ c. "The lives of the captives were now in direct jeopardy, and Fujimori was not going to stand for it."

3. From the statements below, choose those that you believe the author would agree with.

☐ a. Alberto Fujimori acted rashly and carelessly when he ordered the attack on the house.

☒ b. Alberto Fujimori made a difficult but correct decision about how to bring an end to the hostage crisis.

☐ c. If he had a second chance, this time Alberto Fujimori would decide not to attack the house.

4. Choose the statement below that is the weakest argument for meeting violence with violence.

☐ a. Violence can bring a quick, clear end to a difficult situation.

☒ b. Violent people understand and respect violence.

☐ c. Innocent people could be wounded or killed in the crossfire.

_____ Number of correct answers

Record your personal assessment of your work on the Critical Thinking Chart on page 136.

Summarizing and Paraphrasing

Follow the directions provided for questions 1 and 2.

1. Look for the important ideas and events in paragraphs 7 and 8. Summarize those paragraphs in one or two sentences.

The place was bugged
& the rebels were
clueless.

2. Complete the following one-sentence summary of the article using the lettered phrases from the phrase bank below. Write the letters on the lines.

Phrase Bank:

a. a description of the ambassador's party

b. the rescue and Fujimori's final announcement

c. how terrorists held the VIPs hostage and the president of Peru's secret plans for their rescue

The article about "Rescue in Peru" begins with ___a___, goes on to explain ___c___, and ends with ___b___.

_____ Number of correct answers

Record your personal assessment of your work on the Critical Thinking Chart on page 136.

Critical Thinking

Put an X in the box next to the correct answer for questions 1, 2, and 5. Follow the directions provided for the other questions.

1. Which of the following statements from the article is an opinion rather than a fact?

☐ a. "The Japanese ambassador to Peru hosted a gala event on December 17, 1996."

☒ b. "Faced with such a determined foe, the rebels never stood a chance."

☐ c. "In March the rebels found out about the tunnels and moved to the second floor."

2. From what Fujimori said, you can predict that he will

☐ a. regret his actions toward the terrorists.

☑ b. be proud of his record as a tough leader who won't give in to terrorists.

☐ c. be easier on terrorists the next time they become active.

3. Choose from the letters below to correctly complete the following statement. Write the letters on the lines.

On the positive side, ___b___, but on the negative side ___c___.

a. the army's attack began around half past 3 o'clock on April 22

b. most of the hostages were saved

c. one hostage was shot and died later of a heart attack

4. Read paragraph 2. Then choose from the letters below to correctly complete the following statement. Write the letters on the lines.

According to paragraph 2, ___a___ happened because ___b___.

a. about 450 rebels had been jailed

b. many of the rebels were teenagers

c. the hostage crisis at the ambassador's house

5. What did you have to do to answer question 4?

☐ a. find an opinion (what someone thinks about something)

☐ b. find a description (how something looks)

☑ c. find a cause (why something happened)

_____ Number of correct answers

Record your personal assessment of your work on the Critical Thinking Chart on page 136.

Personal Response

What new question do you have about this topic?

_____

_____

_____

_____

Self-Assessment

While reading the article, I found it easiest to

_____

_____

_____

_____

CRITICAL THINKING

TRAGEDY AND RESCUE AT SEA

They were big," recalled Donald Blum, a crew member of the doomed USS *Indianapolis*. "And they had lots of teeth and they swam by with their mouths open…. That scared me about as badly as anything ever has." Blum was talking about sharks—the sharks that surrounded him and his shipmates after their ship sank at sea.

2   The fate of the USS *Indianapolis* is one of the most heartbreaking tales from World War II. The ship and its captain, Charles Butler McVay, had performed admirably during World War II. By late July of 1945, the end of the war was only days away. The ship had just been to an island in the Pacific to deliver a top secret cargo that would crush Japan—fuel and key parts for making two atomic bombs. Mission accomplished, the ship headed for the Philippines. It would never get there.

3   Just after midnight on July 30, 1945, two Japanese torpedoes slammed into the heavy cruiser. There were 1,196 men on board the *Indianapolis* at the time. The explosions caught most of them sleeping.

Two Japanese torpedoes struck the USS Indianapolis *two days before the end of World War II. The ship sank within 12 minutes and 880 men lost their lives.*

Luckily, the tropical night was hot, and many men had chosen to sleep on the deck. These men were not trapped below as some others were.

4   The two torpedoes scored a direct hit. They knocked out all forms of communication. No SOS signal could be sent. The ship was so badly damaged there was little time to launch the lifeboats. More precious time was lost when Captain McVay at first refused to give the order to abandon ship. "We had only about a three degree list," he later testified. "We had been through a hit before [and] we were able to control it quite easily. In my mind, I was not at all perturbed."

5   But within two or three minutes, Captain McVay got a damage report from his executive officer. "We are definitely going down!" the officer told McVay. Realizing that he couldn't save the ship, McVay gave the order to abandon ship.

6   From the time it was hit, the ship took only 12 minutes to sink. About 400 men went down with her. The rest of the crew, many badly wounded, either slipped off the tilting deck or jumped into the sea. Most had just enough time to grab a life jacket.

7   After recovering from the shock of abandoning ship, the men felt certain they would soon be rescued. But they were wrong. Because the *Indianapolis* had

been on a secret mission, the ship hadn't been sending out reports of its position. After all, the enemy might have been listening. In addition, no distress signal had been given. So when the *Indianapolis* didn't appear on time, no rescue search was launched. In all the chaos of the war, no one seemed to notice the missing ship.

8   Meanwhile, the survivors were bobbing around with just their life jackets to protect them in the middle of the Pacific Ocean. They had no food or fresh water. Hour after hour, they floated under

Sharks attacked many men who survived the attack on the Indianapolis *as they floated in the Pacific Ocean waiting to be rescued.*

the blistering sun. The salt water ate at their wounds. Many became sick from swallowing salt water mixed with oil. And beginning with sunrise that first morning, the men faced an additional danger: hungry sharks. When sharks began circling the area, the men swam close together in tight groups to protect themselves. They hit the water with cupped hands and kicked with their feet, hoping to scare the creatures away.

9   These tactics did little good. The sharks kept coming. They would appear in the early morning and again at sunset—their feeding times. One by one, the predator sharks picked off the floating men. The survivors watched helplessly each time a fin disappeared below the surface. That sight meant a shark was moving in for the kill. Who would be the next victim? For a moment, there would be silence—then the men would hear a scream and they would know the answer. No one knows for sure how many men the sharks killed. One survivor put the number between 60 and 80.

10   While some men were killed by sharks, others died from their wounds. And more died after going insane from the endless fear combined with a lack of sleep and no fresh water. In their insanity, these men saw things that weren't there. One man believed he would find a drinking

fountain underwater. He dove down and never resurfaced. Another man thought he saw a ship and swam off, thinking he would meet it. Other men just gave up. "I'll see you, good buddies," one man told his companions. Then he swam off and was gone.

11   Somehow, though, hundreds of other men managed to cling to life. They hung on through the pain and fear and despair. Some cursed, some prayed, some spent their energies trying to cheer up their companions. Again and again their eyes turned to the sky, searching in vain for a rescue plane. It was a trial that only those who survived can fully understand. "It was a horror," said Gabe George. "I took [it] day by day, hour by hour. If they told me I'd have to do this, I would shoot myself. If I knew what was coming I could not have survived."

12   Another survivor described it this way: "it would have been easier to die."

13   The men spent four days and five nights drifting in the water. By then, without water to drink, they were all near death. But their will to live paid off. By chance, a U.S. Navy patrol plane spotted the men. The pilot wiggled the plane's wings to let the men know he had seen them in the vast sea below. He ordered his crew to drop a rubber raft and anything else that might aid the men in the water.

He radioed their location back to the Philippines and the next morning—at last—rescue ships arrived. Three hundred sixteen men survived the ordeal. Eight hundred eighty others didn't. It was the worst wartime loss of life at sea in U.S. Navy history.

14   Most of the survivors were in terrible shape and had to be hospitalized. A few actually had broken bones in their feet from pushing away sharks. Donald Blum was the only one strong enough to climb a rope ladder unaided. Once on board the rescue ship, he headed straight for the drinking fountain. "And I drank and I drank and I drank." 🍂

If you have been timed while reading this article, enter your reading time below. Then turn to the Words-per-Minute Table on page 133 and look up your reading speed (words per minute). Enter your reading speed on the graph on page 134.

Reading Time: Lesson 11

_3_ : _4 7_

Minutes   Seconds

READING COMPREHENSION

103

A Finding the Main Idea

One statement below expresses the main idea of the article. One statement is too general, or too broad. The other statement explains only part of the article; it is too narrow. Label the statements using the following key:

M—Main Idea   **B—Too Broad**   **N—Too Narrow**

_M_   1. When a U.S. Navy ship was torpedoed and sank just before the end of World War II, its survivors had to face hungry sharks.

_N_   2. At first the captain of the USS *Indianapolis* couldn't believe that his ship was actually going down, and he delayed giving the order to abandon ship.

_B_   3. Shark attack is a terrible danger for shipwreck survivors in the warm Pacific Ocean.

_____ Score 15 points for a correct M answer.

_____ Score 5 points for each correct B or N answer.

_____ **Total Score:** Finding the Main Idea

B Recalling Facts

How well do you remember the facts in the article? Put an X in the box next to the answer that correctly completes each statement about the article.

1. The USS *Indianapolis*'s last mission was to
   - ☒ a. conduct spy activities.
   - ☐ b. sink Japanese warships.
   - ☒ c. deliver fuel and key parts for making atomic bombs.

2. The *Indianapolis* was sunk by
   - ☒ a. direct hits by two Japanese torpedoes.
   - ☐ b. a bomb dropped from an airplane.
   - ☐ c. the sudden explosion of a bomb that it was transporting.

3. The time between the moment the ship was hit and the moment it sank was only
   - ☒ a. 12 minutes.
   - ☐ b. 4 minutes.
   - ☐ c. three hours.

4. The greatest danger the survivors faced in the water was
   - ☐ a. sunburn.
   - ☒ b. hungry sharks.
   - ☐ c. nausea.

5. The floating survivors were finally spotted by a
   - ☒ a. U.S. Navy patrol plane.
   - ☐ b. passing cruise ship.
   - ☐ c. Japanese warship.

Score 5 points for each correct answer.

_____ **Total Score:** Recalling Facts

C | Making Inferences

When you combine your own experience and information from a text to draw a conclusion that is not directly stated in that text, you are making an inference. Below are five statements that may or may not be inferences based on information in the article. Label the statements using the following key:

C—Correct Inference   **F—Faulty Inference**

F 1. Captain McVay survived the tragedy.

C 2. Some people felt that Captain McVay should have given the order to abandon ship sooner.

F 3. The *Indianapolis* was carrying too many sailors for its size.

F 4. Sharks are easily frightened away by loud noises and irregular movements.

C 5. By staying together, the men increased their chances of being spotted by a passing airplane.

Score 5 points for each correct answer.

_____ **Total Score:** Making Inferences

D | Using Words Precisely

Each numbered sentence below contains an underlined word or phrase from the article. Following the sentence are three definitions. One definition is closest to the meaning of the underlined word. One definition is opposite or nearly opposite. Label those two definitions using the following key. Do not label the remaining definition.

C—Closest   **O—Opposite or Nearly Opposite**

1. "We had only about a three degree <u>list</u>," he later testified.

   O a. tilt

   _____ b. burn

   C c. upright position

2. "In my mind, I was not at all <u>perturbed</u>."

   O a. calm

   C b. troubled or upset

   _____ c. interested

3. One by one, the <u>predator</u> sharks picked off the men.

   O a. relating to one who is attacked or devoured by another

   _____ b. relating to one who warns another of an attack

   C c. relating to one who attacks and devours another

4. Again and again their eyes turned to the sky, searching <u>in vain</u> for a rescue plane.

   O a. successfully

   C b. uselessly

   _____ c. painfully

5. The pilot wiggled the plane's wings to let the men know he had seen them in the <u>vast</u> sea below.

_____ a. enormous

_____ b. cold

_____ c. small

_____ Score 3 points for each correct C answer.

_____ Score 2 points for each correct O answer.

_____ **Total Score:** Using Words Precisely

Enter the four total scores in the spaces below, and add them together to find your Reading Comprehension Score. Then record your score on the graph on page 135.

Score	Question Type	Lesson 11
_____	Finding the Main Idea	
_____	Recalling Facts	
_____	Making Inferences	
_____	Using Words Precisely	
_____	**Reading Comprehension Score**	

Author's Approach

Put an X in the box next to the correct answer.

1. The main purpose of the first paragraph is to

☐ a. inform the reader about the habits of sharks.

☑ b. introduce the reader to the problem faced by the *Indianapolis* crew members.

☐ c. describe the people who were floating in the sea.

2. What does the author imply by saying "Many [survivors] became sick from swallowing salt water mixed with oil"?

☐ a. All seawater is a combination of salt water and oil.

☑ b. Oil from the sunken *Indianapolis* was still present in the seawater that surrounded the survivors.

☐ c. The Japanese torpedoes had contained oil.

3. The author tells this story mainly by

☑ a. relating events in the order they happened.

☐ b. comparing different topics.

☐ c. using his or her imagination and creativity.

_____ Number of correct answers

Record your personal assessment of your work on the Critical Thinking Chart on page 136.

Summarizing and Paraphrasing

Put an X in the box next to the correct answer for question 1. Follow the directions provided for these question 2.

1. Below are summaries of the article. Choose the summary that says all the most important things about the article but in the fewest words.

☐ a. The crew members who survived the sinking of the USS *Indianapolis* were most likely the ones who had been sleeping on the deck. They were not trapped below as some men were. After the boat sank, the men faced additional dangers.

☐ b. Just before the end of World War II, the USS *Indianapolis* was on its way back from a successful mission. It had just delivered materials necessary for making atomic bombs. Suddenly, two Japanese torpedoes hit it. Many men were sleeping below decks and most of them drowned.

☒ c. The USS *Indianapolis*, after completing a secret mission toward the end of World War II, was torpedoed and sank quickly. Altogether, 880 men died as a result of the Japanese attack, and 316 survived attacks by hungry sharks until they were finally rescued.

2. Reread paragraph 6 in the article. Below, write a summary of the paragraph in no more than 25 words.

The ship sank quickly.

Reread your summary and decide whether it covers the important ideas in the paragraph. Next, decide how to shorten the summary to 15 words or less without leaving out any essential information. Write this summary below.

_____

_____

_____

_____ Number of correct answers

Record your personal assessment of your work on the Critical Thinking Chart on page 136.

Critical Thinking

Put an X in the box next to the correct answer for questions 1, 2, and 5. Follow the directions provided for the other questions.

1. Which of the following statements from the article is an opinion rather than a fact?

☒ a. "The fate of the USS *Indianapolis* is one of the most heartbreaking tales from World War II."

☐ b. "There were 1,196 men on board the USS *Indianapolis* at the time."

☐ c. "Three hundred sixteen men survived the ordeal."

2. From the article, you can predict that if there had been time to load the crew into lifeboats,

☐ a. more men would have died.

☐ b. the danger of shark attack would have increased for the survivors.

☒ c. more men would have survived.

3. Choose from the letters below to correctly complete the following statement. Write the letters on the lines.

In the article, ___A___ and ___C___ are alike.

a. the fate of Donald Blum

b. the fate of those who went down with the ship

c. the fate of Gabe George

4. Read paragraph 7. Then choose from the letters below to correctly complete the following statement. Write the letters on the lines.

According to paragraph 7, ___C___ because ___a___.

a. the *Indianapolis* had been on a secret mission and hadn't sent out any distress signal

b. the men were sure they would be rescued soon

c. no one was looking for survivors of the *Indianapolis*

5. How is the story related to the theme of this book?

☐ a. Survivors of the sinking of a U.S. Navy ship had to fight sharks, thirst, and hunger.

☐ b. Japanese torpedoes sank a U.S. Navy ship, killing at least 400 men.

☒ c. Survivors of the sinking of a U.S. Navy ship were saved from almost certain death after floating in the sea for days.

_____ Number of correct answers

Record your personal assessment of your work on the Critical Thinking Chart on page 136.

Personal Response

If I were the author, I would change

_____

_____

_____

_____

Self-Assessment

The part I found most difficult about the article was

_____

_____

_____

_____

I found this difficult because

_____

_____

_____

_____

_____

CRITICAL THINKING

LOST IN THE MOUNTAINS

Dee Dubin is carried off a helicopter after she was rescued from the backcountry southwest of Aspen, Colorado.

They knew the dangers before they left. The forecasts called for severe blizzards and also, possibly, avalanches. Still, a group of four men and three women decided to go cross-country skiing in the Colorado mountains. They felt sure they could handle any storm that might blow up. After all, they were fine skiers. Some of them had already survived fierce winter storms in the mountains. And the avalanche danger? "There is always an avalanche danger on this route," said Elliot Brown, one of the skiers. To them, this ski trip was just another wilderness adventure.

2 Not everyone agreed with that assessment. Some people thought the group was nuts. Doug Bitterman, manager of the local ski touring center, saw the skiers head out. Shaking his head, he cracked, "That's going to be the Rescue of the Year."

3 Bitterman didn't know how right he was. When the skiers took off on Friday, February 19, 1993, they were heading into the most frightening and dangerous experience of their lives. They departed from Ashcroft, Colorado, and headed for a hut about seven miles up Express Creek.

The skiers, who ranged in age from 34 to 50, began their trek late in the morning. For such an experienced group, they did not plan their trip very well. Only two of their sleeping bags were waterproof. They brought no insulated sleeping pads and no tent.

4 It wasn't long before the winds began to howl and the snow began to fall. Still, the group pressed ahead. Slowly, however, their confidence began to sag. "We were in snow that was knee deep, at times waist deep," said Rob Dubin later. "One minute you could see ahead and the next you couldn't see the tips of your skis." Only after they had gone too far to turn back did they realize exactly how much danger they were in. At that point, Brown said, "we couldn't do anything about it anymore."

5 Blinded by the snow, the group lost the trail and turned the wrong way. Now they had no chance of reaching the safety of the hut. Night fell, and the temperature plunged to below zero. The skiers tried to construct a snow cave for shelter, but it soon collapsed because the snow was too dry and fluffy. So the seven skiers spent a sleepless night huddled together in a hole they dug in the snow. By early morning they were all cold, wet, and tired.

6 At this point, the skiers couldn't agree on their next move. Should they stay put or move on? Should they remain together or split up? The two strongest skiers, Ken Torp and Elliot Brown, suggested a difficult route as their best bet back to Express Creek. Richard Rost protested, saying it would be too hard for the women. Rost believed they would be better off retracing their steps. In the end, Torp and Brown headed out on their own. If the route was impassable, they said, they would return in 25 minutes. If they didn't come back, the rest should follow them.

7 Torp and Brown didn't return. The three women and the two men waited for more than an hour but then decided not to follow the same trail. Instead, they took Rost's advice and headed back toward Ashcroft. Initially, Rost and Rob Dubin led the way. But 50-year-old Brigitte Schluger began falling behind. Her tiny body was no match for the elements. "She was falling," recalled Dubin, "getting blown over by the wind."

8 Dubin wanted to slow down for Schluger's sake, but Rost resisted. Rost feared that Andrea Brett, his girlfriend, might freeze to death if she slowed down. At last, Rost and Brett went off on their own while Dubin, his wife, Dee, and Schluger continued at a slower pace. The first rule of mountaineering is to stay together. The skiers had now broken that commandment twice.

9 After seven grueling hours, Rost and Brett made it back safely to Ashcroft. By then it was late Saturday afternoon. They told rescue workers about their five lost companions, broken into two groups. Starting the next day, searchers braved a

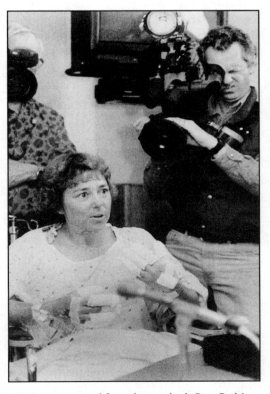

Having recovered from her ordeal, Dee Dubin talks to reporters during a news conference at a Denver hospital.

series of blizzards to look for the lost skiers. For two days, rescuers searched the mountains. As time passed, however, hope slowly drained away. By Tuesday morning it looked doubtful that any of the five would ever be found alive. Sheriff Bob Braudis began to worry about the safety of the rescuers. "We are using real, live rescuers," he said, "to search for probable dead bodies."

10   Actually—against all odds—the five skiers were still alive. Torp and Brown had spent a miserable Saturday night. Brown's sleeping bag was very wet and provided no insulation. To keep from freezing to death, the two men forced themselves to stay awake all night, talking and flexing their muscles. The following day they got lucky. They stumbled upon an unlocked cabin owned by the Bureau of Land Management (BLM). As Brown later put it, "that was a lifesaver."

11   The two men spent Sunday night in the cabin. They built a fire in the stove, using it to melt snow for drinking water and to dry out their sleeping bags. The next morning, despite the continuing bad weather, the two men decided to leave the cabin. They felt that the storm would prevent anyone from rescuing them, so they pledged to save themselves. Before leaving the cabin, they stamped the word HELP in the snow and hung an American flag upside down—a distress signal. Torp also left a note just in case anyone else came to the cabin. The note read, "Our plan is to ski all the way to Taylor Park Res. on 2/22. The snow is deep. The trail

unpacked…. We have food for one day. We apologize for using the cabin."

12   The situation for the Dubins and Schluger, meanwhile, was even grimmer. The three were completely lost. The two women had grown very weak and were suffering from severe frostbite. Snow had fallen into Dee Dubin's boot, numbing her feet. "I woke her up 30 times during the night and told her to flex her fingers and toes so they wouldn't freeze," Rob Dubin later said. Unable to carry her backpack or her sopping wet sleeping bag, Schluger had just dropped them along the trail. For two nights she used Dee Dubin's sleeping bag, while Dee shared her husband's.

13   Then, on Monday morning, something miraculous happened. The Dubins and Schluger stumbled onto the very same cabin that Torp and Brown had found. Seeing Torp's note, they figured the two men were still alive and in pretty good shape. Incredibly, Schluger and the Dubins had arrived at the cabin just two hours after Torp and Brown left it.

14   Torp and Brown had used all the firewood, so Rob Dubin broke up the furniture and burned it. He knew this cabin was their last hope. They would never be able to ski out on their own like Torp and Brown. They would just have to wait and hope to be rescued.

15   On Tuesday morning, Torp and Brown made it to Taylor Park Reservoir. There they ran into some snowmobilers. "Are you the two lost guys?" asked one snowmobiler.

16   "Yes!" they both shouted.

17   Torp and Brown were overjoyed to be rescued, but their happiness was clouded by thoughts of the friends they had left back on the mountain. They heard that a helicopter had spotted Schluger's blue backpack and sleeping bag. To Torp, that evidence meant Schluger and the Dubins had probably died in an avalanche. Rescuers thought the same thing. They had scoured the region on skis, snowshoes, snowmobiles, planes, and helicopters and had found nothing.

18   A lot of snow had fallen since the skiers had started out the previous Friday, and now another storm was moving in. There was just enough clear weather to give the rescue effort one more try. And so the rescuers headed out again. Luckily, a helicopter pilot saw some tracks in the snow. The tracks led to the BLM hut. The pilot landed in a snowfield nearby and moments later, he radioed the good news: "We have all three." 🍃

If you have been timed while reading this article, enter your reading time below. Then turn to the Words-per-Minute Table on page 133 and look up your reading speed (words per minute). Enter your reading speed on the graph on page 134.

Reading Time: Lesson 12

_4_ : _31_
Minutes   *Seconds*

A Finding the Main Idea

One statement below expresses the main idea of the article. One statement is too general, or too broad. The other statement explains only part of the article; it is too narrow. Label the statements using the following key:

M—Main Idea　　　**B—Too Broad**　　　**N—Too Narrow**

_M_ 1. Seven skiers foolishly ignored severe weather warnings and ended up needing to be rescued in the Colorado mountains.

_B_ 2. Experienced skiers should be smart enough to respect nature and prepare for bad weather.

_N_ 3. At one point in their ordeal, the lost skiers broke up into two groups, with two skiers choosing a more difficult path to safety.

_____ Score 15 points for a correct M answer.

_____ Score 5 points for each correct B or N answer.

_____ **Total Score:** Finding the Main Idea

B Recalling Facts

How well do you remember the facts in the article? Put an X in the box next to the answer that correctly completes each statement about the article.

1. Before the skiers left, they heard weather forecasts calling for
☐ a. tornadoes.
☐ b. ice storms.
☒ c. severe blizzards and possible avalanches.

2. The skiers spent the first night in
☐ a. tents they had brought along.
☒ b. a hole they had dug in the snow.
☐ c. a snow cave.

3. The first skiers to make it back to safety were
☒ a. Rost and Brett.
☐ b. the Dubins and Schluger.
☐ c. Torp and Brown.

4. Torp and Brown spent one night in a cabin owned by the
☐ a. National Park Service.
☒ b. Bureau of Land Management.
☐ c. Colorado Division of Wildlife.

5. The breakthrough in finding the last three skiers happened when a helicopter pilot spotted
☐ a. smoke rising from the hut where they were staying.
☐ b. the word HELP stamped into the snow.
☒ c. Schluger and the Dubins' tracks in the snow.

Score 5 points for each correct answer.

_____ **Total Score:** Recalling Facts

C | Making Inferences

When you combine your own experience and information from a text to draw a conclusion that is not directly stated in that text, you are making an inference. Below are five statements that may or may not be inferences based on information in the article. Label the statements using the following key:

C—Correct Inference   F—Faulty Inference

_____ 1. When bad weather is forecast, skiers who venture out are breaking the law.

_____ 2. No one could have guessed that the seven skiers' adventure could become dangerous.

_____ 3. Rescuers risked their own safety to find the skiers.

_____ 4. Without persistence and courage, the skiers might have died.

_____ 5. Once a sleeping bag becomes wet, it loses its ability to keep the user warm.

Score 5 points for each correct answer.

_____ **Total Score:** Making Inferences

D | Using Words Precisely

Each numbered sentence below contains an underlined word or phrase from the article. Following the sentence are three definitions. One definition is closest to the meaning of the underlined word. One definition is opposite or nearly opposite. Label those two definitions using the following key. Do not label the remaining definition.

C—Closest   O—Opposite or Nearly Opposite

1. Night fell, and the temperature <u>plunged</u> to below zero.

_____ a. moved

_____ b. rose

_____ c. fell quickly

2. After seven <u>grueling</u> hours, Rost and Brett made it back safely to Ashcroft.

_____ a. energizing

_____ b. exhausting

_____ c. long

3. They felt that the storm would prevent anyone from rescuing them, so they <u>pledged</u> to save themselves.

_____ a. vowed

_____ b. began

_____ c. refused

4. Then, on Monday morning, something <u>miraculous</u> happened.

_____ a. marvelous

_____ b. ordinary

_____ c. embarrassing

5. They had <u>scoured</u> the region on skis, snowshoes, snowmobiles,…and had found nothing.

_____ a. cleared

___C___ b. searched carefully

___O___ c. hardly bothered to look at

_____ Score 3 points for each correct C answer.

_____ Score 2 points for each correct O answer.

_____ **Total Score:** Using Words Precisely

Enter the four total scores in the spaces below, and add them together to find your Reading Comprehension Score. Then record your score on the graph on page 135.

Score	Question Type	Lesson 12
_____	Finding the Main Idea	
_____	Recalling Facts	
_____	Making Inferences	
_____	Using Words Precisely	
_____	**Reading Comprehension Score**	

Author's Approach

Put an X in the box next to the correct answer.

1. The author uses the first sentence of the article to

☐ a. inform the reader about winter weather in the mountains.

☐ b. describe the qualities of cross-country skiing.

☒ c. hint at the trouble that was on its way.

2. From the statements below, choose those that you believe the author would agree with.

☒ a. The seven skiers made a mistake when they split up.

☒ b. The seven skiers should not have ignored the severe weather warnings.

☐ c. The storm that overtook the skiers was not particularly harsh.

3. In this article, "Shaking his head, he [the manager of the ski touring center] cracked, 'That's going to be the Rescue of the Year'" means

☒ a. The manager could tell that the skiers were making a mistake by heading up the mountain in spite of a bad weather forecast.

☐ b. The manager could predict the future accurately.

☐ c. The manager hoped that the skiers would run into trouble.

4. The author probably wrote this article in order to

☒ a. tell the story of a near-tragedy and an exciting rescue.

☐ b. make readers afraid to ski in Colorado.

☐ c. prove that men are better skiers than women.

_____ Number of correct answers

Record your personal assessment of your work on the Critical Thinking Chart on page 136.

CRITICAL THINKING

Summarizing and Paraphrasing

Follow the directions provided for question 1. Put an X in the box next to the correct answer for question 2.

1. Look for the important ideas and events in paragraphs 13 and 14. Summarize those paragraphs in one or two sentences.

   They had been in the same hut.

2. Read the statement about the article below. Then read the paraphrase of that statement. Choose the reason that best tells why the paraphrase does not say the same thing as the statement.

   Statement: Torp and Brown were overjoyed to be rescued, but their happiness was clouded by thoughts of the friends they had left back on the mountain.

   Paraphrase: Torp and Brown were so happy to be rescued that they totally forgot about the friends they had abandoned on the mountain.

   ☐ a. Paraphrase says too much.

   ☐ b. Paraphrase doesn't say enough.

   ☒ c. Paraphrase doesn't agree with the statement about the article.

   _____ Number of correct answers

   Record your personal assessment of your work on the Critical Thinking Chart on page 136.

Critical Thinking

Put an X in the box next to the correct answer for question 1. Follow the directions provided for the other questions.

1. From what the article told about the skiers' lack of camping equipment, you can predict that if they go on another overnight skiing trip, they will

   ☐ a. bring waterproof sleeping bags and tents only if bad weather is predicted.

   ☐ b. again put their trust in their ability to do without the equipment.

   ☒ c. bring waterproof sleeping bags and tents in case of emergency.

2. Choose from the letters below to correctly complete the following statement. Write the letters on the lines.

   On the positive side, ___a___, but on the negative side ___b___.

   a. all seven skiers survived the ordeal

   b. a great deal of time and effort was spent to rescue people who had been thoughtless and reckless

   c. four men and three women went on a cross-country skiing trip

3. Think about cause-effect relationships in the article. Fill in the blanks in the cause-effect chart, drawing from the letters below.

Cause	Effect
Severe weather was forecast.	_C_
Heavy snow began to fall.	_A_
_B_	Her feet became numb.

   a. The skiers lost their way.

   b. Snow had fallen into Dee Dubin's boot.

   c. Doug Bitterman predicted that the skiers would need to be rescued.

4. Which paragraphs from the article provide evidence that supports your answer to question 3?

_____ 12 _____

_____ Number of correct answers

Record your personal assessment of your work on the Critical Thinking Chart on page 136.

The part I found most difficult about the article was

_____

_____

_____

_____

I found this difficult because

_____

_____

_____

_____

Personal Response

How do you think you would feel if you had been the first skier to reach safety and you knew that your friends were still lost?

_____

_____

_____

THE HEROES OF PEA ISLAND

It is called the "Graveyard of the Atlantic." Warm Gulf Stream water hits the cold Labrador Current, causing treacherous currents. Perilous shoals and sandbars lace the shallow water. Winds whip up wild waves. The weather is anyone's guess. Hundreds of ships have fallen prey to these hazards. This nasty stretch of ocean along the coast of North Carolina has earned its nickname.

2   Even today these waters demand respect. One hundred years ago the dangers were even greater. Without modern navigational equipment, ships had to hug the coastline. But that course of action left little room for error. A slight mistake in navigating or a sudden storm could quickly drive a ship aground on one of the shoals or sandbars. There, powerful winds and waves would smash the trapped vessel to pieces. Sailors who tried to swim through the undertows to shore rarely made it. Those who stayed with the ship, on the other hand, often died a slow death from exhaustion.

3   In response to this danger, the government set up the U.S. Life-Saving Service in 1848. (Later, combined with the Revenue

Richard Etheridge (far left) and the Pea Island lifesaving crew pose in front of the Pea Island Station.

Cutter Service, it became the United States Coast Guard.) The government set up life-saving stations along the East and West Coasts as well as on the Great Lakes. The men at these stations, called surfmen, patrolled up and down the shore. Their job was to spot and rescue survivors of shipwrecks. Each day the crews performed drills to sharpen their skills. Over the years, they saved thousands of lives.

4   Twenty-nine life-saving stations were built along the coast of North Carolina alone. One was at Pea Island. This station was unlike any other. It was the only one run solely by African Americans. In those days, blacks were rarely given the chance to shoulder such duties. But in 1880, Lieutenant Charles Shoemaker set up the all-black unit. He chose an African American named Richard Etheridge to be in charge of the station. "[Etheridge] is reputed one of the best surfmen on this part of the coast of North Carolina," Shoemaker wrote. Shoemaker suggested that the rest of the crew be African-American, as well.

The lifesaving crew at work at the Pea Island station around 1910

5 Shoemaker's move was a bold one. It was also smart. The crew at Pea Island proved to be as brave and as talented as any group around. Again and again, their courage was put to the test. They made dozens of rescues over the years. The most spectacular one occurred on October 11, 1896.

6 On that night, the schooner *E. S. Newman* was on its way to Virginia from Connecticut. One quick look at a map shows the ship shouldn't have ended up off the coast of North Carolina. But a terrifying storm blew the vessel 100 miles off course. Winds drove the ship aground just two miles from the Pea Island station. To the nine people aboard the *Newman*, death seemed certain. They had only one last hope—maybe someone would see their distress flare.

7 And indeed, through the driving rain, surfman Theodore Meekins spotted the flare. He alerted the six other men who were on duty with him. Together they rushed to mount a rescue. Using mules to haul their equipment, they hurried down to the beach. But the sea was far too wild for them to use their lifeboat. Richard Etheridge later wrote in his log, "It seemed impossible under such unfavorable conditions to render any assistance."

8 Then he hit on a daring idea. Why not tie two of the surfmen to a rope and have them swim out to the wreck with a lifeline? It would be risky and it might not work, but it was worth a try. Under a pitch-black sky, two surfmen quickly lashed themselves together. They plunged into the restless sea and fought their way through the waves and undertow. Somehow, they managed to reach the disabled ship. Then they brought the passengers, one by one, through the turbulent surf and back to shore. Among those saved were the captain, his wife, and their three-year-old son.

9 The crew at Pea Island never received any recognition for their heroism. No one can say for sure why these men were never honored. Perhaps it was racism. Perhaps, as one of the crew's descendants said, "It was just one of those things." In any case, for many years their exploits lived on only in the stories of relatives and friends.

10 That situation changed in 1995. Four people joined forces to seek recognition for the Pea Island crew. Stephen Rochon, a black Coast Guard commander, discovered the history of the crew while doing research for Black History month. Two college students, David Zoby and David Wright, stumbled across the story while traveling through North Carolina. Then there was a 14-year-old white North Carolina high school student named Kate Burkart. She had seen a slide show that Zoby and Wright produced about the rescue. They all, in their own way, felt that the crew should be honored for its work. Burkart even wrote Jesse Helms, her U.S. senator, for help.

11 Their combined efforts paid off. In 1995, the U.S. Coast Guard approved a posthumous Gold Lifesaving Medal for each of the seven members of the Pea Island crew. In addition to Meekins and Etheridge, the crew members were Benjamin Bowser, Louis Wescott, Dorman Pugh, Stanley Wise, and William Irving.

12 On March 5, 1996, a ceremony was held at the Navy Memorial in Washington, D.C. (It was the first time the four supporters of the award had gotten together.) Speaking at that time, Kate Burkart said, "The deeds of the Pea Island crew stand as a symbol of our attempt to honor all the nameless sacrifices that have gone before us regardless of religion, politics, or race."

13 Many descendants of the crew attended the ceremony. One was Coast Guard Captain Dwight Meekins. He didn't want people to focus on the delay of one hundred years. He stressed the positive. "[March 5]," he said, "was a good day for...the old Pea Island crew, the descendants, and the Coast Guard." ✍

If you have been timed while reading this article, enter your reading time below. Then turn to the Words-per-Minute Table on page 133 and look up your reading speed (words per minute). Enter your reading speed on the graph on page 134.

Reading Time: Lesson 13

_____ : 54

Minutes   Seconds

A | Finding the Main Idea

One statement below expresses the main idea of the article. One statement is too general, or too broad. The other statement explains only part of the article; it is too narrow. Label the statements using the following key:

M—Main Idea   **B—Too Broad**   **N—Too Narrow**

_B_   1. To combat the disasters that can happen at sea, it is a good idea to set up life-saving organizations on the coast.

_N_   2. The African-American life-saving crew at Pea Island was responsible for dozens of sea rescues, including one famous rescue for which the crew was formally recognized.

_M_   3. On October 11, 1896, the surfmen rescued the nine people aboard a boat that had run aground in a terrible storm.

_____ Score 15 points for a correct M answer.

_____ Score 5 points for each correct B or N answer.

_____ **Total Score:** Finding the Main Idea

B | Recalling Facts

How well do you remember the facts in the article? Put an X in the box next to the answer that correctly completes each statement about the article.

1. The nickname "Graveyard of the Atlantic" has been given to the stretch of ocean along the coast of
   ☐ a. Georgia.
   ☒ b. North Carolina.
   ☐ c. Florida.

2. The government set up the U.S. Life-Saving Service in
   ☒ a. 1848.
   ☐ b. 1783.
   ☐ c. 1912.

3. The life-saving station at Pea Island was different from the rest because
   ☐ a. it was located in North Carolina.
   ☒ b. it was staffed entirely by African Americans.
   ☐ c. its surfmen were skilled and daring.

4. The crew couldn't used their lifeboat to rescue the _Newman_ because
   ☐ a. they couldn't find it.
   ☐ b. the boat had been badly damaged.
   ☒ c. the sea was too rough for the small boat.

5. Each member of the crew of the life-saving station at Pea Island received a
   ☐ a. Purple Heart.
   ☐ b. Congressional Medal of Honor.
   ☒ c. Gold Lifesaving Medal.

Score 5 points for each correct answer.

_____ **Total Score:** Recalling Facts

C | Making Inferences

When you combine your own experience and information from a text to draw a conclusion that is not directly stated in that text, you are making an inference. Below are five statements that may or may not be inferences based on information in the article. Label the statements using the following key:

C—Correct Inference   **F—Faulty Inference**

_C_ 1. Many lives were lost to storms and dangerous currents along the Atlantic coast before the life-saving stations were set up.

_C_ 2. The crew at Pea Island were proud of their lifesaving record.

_C_ 3. By tying themselves together, the surfmen believed that they increased their chances of survival and success.

_F_ 4. Before 1996, everyone who ever rescued anyone on the Atlantic coast had been officially thanked except for the crew of Pea Island.

_F_ 5. The Pea Island lifesavers were angry that they never got recognition for their work during their lifetimes.

Score 5 points for each correct answer.

_____ **Total Score:** Making Inferences

D | Using Words Precisely

Each numbered sentence below contains an underlined word or phrase from the article. Following the sentence are three definitions. One definition is closest to the meaning of the underlined word. One definition is opposite or nearly opposite. Label those two definitions using the following key. Do not label the remaining definition.

C—Closest   O—Opposite or Nearly Opposite

1. <u>Perilous</u> shoals and sandbars lace the shallow water.

   _O_ a. safe

   _C_ b. dangerous

   _____ c. rocky

2. Hundreds of ships have fallen prey to these <u>hazards</u>.

   _C_ a. risky conditions

   _____ b. unavoidable conditions

   _O_ c. comfortable and safe conditions

3. Without modern navigational equipment, ships had to <u>hug</u> the coastline.

   _____ a. map

   _C_ b. stay close to

   _O_ c. sail far away from

4. Together they rushed to <u>mount</u> a rescue.

   _C_ a. set up

   _O_ b. prevent

   _____ c. pay for

5. In 1995, the U.S. Coast Guard approved a <u>posthumous</u> Gold Lifesaving Medal for each of the seven members of the Pea Island crew.

_____ a. respected

_____ b. occurring before death

_____ c. occurring after death

_____ Score 3 points for each correct C answer.

_____ Score 2 points for each correct O answer.

_____ **Total Score:** Using Words Precisely

Enter the four total scores in the spaces below, and add them together to find your Reading Comprehension Score. Then record your score on the graph on page 135.

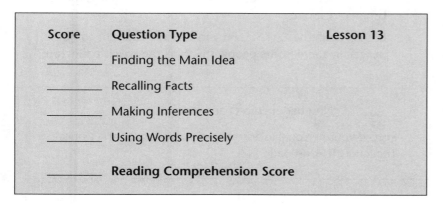

Score	Question Type	Lesson 13
_____	Finding the Main Idea	
_____	Recalling Facts	
_____	Making Inferences	
_____	Using Words Precisely	
_____	**Reading Comprehension Score**	

Author's Approach

Put an X in the box next to the correct answer.

1. The author uses the first sentence of the article to

☒ a. inform the reader about the reputation a particular part of the ocean.

☐ b. compare the Atlantic Ocean and the Pacific Ocean.

☐ c. entertain the reader with humorous wordplay.

2. Which of the following statements from the article best describes the qualities of the Pea Island crew?

☐ a. "In 1995, the U.S. Coast Guard approved a posthumous Gold Lifesaving Medal for each of the seven members of the Pea Island crew."

☐ b. "Under a pitch-black sky, two surfmen quickly lashed themselves together."

☒ c. "The crew at Pea Island proved to be as brave and as talented as any group around."

3. Choose the statement below that best describes the author's position in paragraph 9.

☐ a. The Pea Island crew showed heroism in rescuing the *Newman* and deserved to be recognized for their efforts.

☐ b. Racism was definitely the only reason why few people ever heard about the heroism of the Pea Island crew.

☒ c. Relatives of the Pea Island crew tried for many years to inform the general public about the surfmen's heroism.

4. The author probably wrote this article in order to

☐ a. describe the weather conditions along the Atlantic coast.

☐ b. persuade readers to rescue stranded travelers.

☒ c. spread the story of courageous but overlooked heroes.

_____ Number of correct answers

Record your personal assessment of your work on the Critical Thinking Chart on page 136.

Summarizing and Paraphrasing

Follow the directions provided for questions 1 and 2. Put an X in the box next to the correct answer for question 3.

1. Complete the following one-sentence summary of the article using the lettered phrases from the phrase bank below. Write the letters on the lines.

Phrase Bank:

a. the Pea Island crew and its heroic deeds

b. a description of the stretch of ocean along the North Carolina coast

c. the awarding of medals to the crew in 1995

The article about "The Heroes of Pea Island" begins with_____b_____, goes on to explain_____a_____, and ends with_____c_____.

2. Reread paragraph 4 in the article. Below, write a summary of the paragraph in no more than 25 words.

Describe Pea Island Crew

Reread your summary and decide whether it covers the important ideas in the paragraph. Next, decide how to shorten the summary to 15 words or less without leaving out any essential information. Write this summary below.

3. Choose the best one-sentence paraphrase for the following sentence from the article:

"Warm Gulf Stream water hits the cold Labrador Current, causing treacherous currents."

☒ a. When warm Gulf Stream water collides with the cold Labrador Current, dangerous currents are created.

☐ b. Dangerous currents create the warm Gulf Stream and the cold Labrador Current.

☐ c. Even though the Gulf Stream and Labrador Current combine peacefully there, some people still think the area is dangerous.

_____ Number of correct answers

Record your personal assessment of your work on the Critical Thinking Chart on page 136.

Critical Thinking

Follow the directions provided for these questions.

1. For each statement below, write O if it expresses an opinion or write F if it expresses a fact.

   _F_ a. The U.S. Life-Saving Service later became part of the U.S. Coast Guard.

   _O_ b. The crew of Pea Island should have been thanked more often than they were.

   _F_ c. The Pea Island surfmen rescued the captain of the disabled *Newman*, along with his wife and son.

2. Choose from the letters below to correctly complete the following statement. Write the letters on the lines.

   In the article, ___b___ and ___c___ are alike.

   a. the goal of Kate Burkart

   b. the goal of Stephen Rochon

   c. the goal of Theodore Meekins

3. Choose from the letters below to correctly complete the following statement. Write the letters on the lines.

   According to the article, ___a___ caused the schooner *E. S. Newman* to ___c___, and the effect was ___b___.

   a. a powerful storm

   b. the people aboard were in terrible danger

   c. blow off course and run aground

4. In which paragraph did you find your information or details to answer question 3?

   _____

_____ Number of correct answers

Record your personal assessment of your work on the Critical Thinking Chart on page 136.

Personal Response

What was most surprising or interesting to you about this article?

_____

_____

_____

_____

Self-Assessment

One of the things I did best when reading this article was

_____

_____

_____

I believe I did this well because

_____

_____

_____

THE SINKING OF PT 109

Commander John F. Kennedy aboard PT 109. *Kennedy and his crew patrolled the southwest Pacific Ocean during World War II.*

The dark shape appeared out of nowhere. It was about 250 yards off the starboard bow. At first, the men of *PT 109* thought it was another patrol torpedo (PT) boat. But it was 2:30 in the morning on August 2, 1943. The night sky made it hard to see. Within seconds, the men discovered their mistake. The black shape moving toward them was not another PT boat; it was a Japanese destroyer and it was coming at them at top speed!

2   Lieutenant John F. Kennedy, the future president of the United States, was in command of *PT 109*. He tried to turn his ship to the side in order to fire his torpedoes at the enemy destroyer. He didn't make it. *PT 109* had turned about one-third of the way when the destroyer rammed into it, splitting it in half. Only 10 seconds had elapsed between the time Kennedy saw the destroyer and the moment of impact.

3   *PT 109* was one of many patrol torpedo boats on duty in the Solomon Islands in the Pacific Ocean during World War II. Their job was to disrupt the Japanese nighttime supply convoys

known as the "Tokyo Express." Speedy PT boats were much too small and light to slug it out with enemy destroyers during the day. Instead, they had to attack at night, like mosquitoes, and then quickly dash for cover behind one of the many islands in the region. The PT boat torpedoes, Kennedy once boasted, "[could] sink any ship on the sea." The Japanese feared PT boat attacks, calling the boats "cat-eyed devils." But on this night, the destroyer won. The Japanese captain saw the PT boat first and moved in for the kill. Kennedy and his crew had no chance to get away.

4   The crash killed two of the 13 crew members instantly. Kennedy himself barely missed getting crushed to death by the steel prow of the destroyer. The stern half of the PT boat sank quickly. Kennedy and five others were left on the bow, which was kept afloat by its watertight hold. The sea, however, was ablaze with fire caused by gasoline and flying sparks. Kennedy feared the fire would spread to the bow, causing it to explode, so he ordered his men into the water. Luckily, the inferno stayed away from the bow and slowly died down. After about 15 minutes, Kennedy and a couple of other men returned to the floating hulk.

5   Kennedy then began to call out the names of his missing crew members. He heard several responses from the water. He and the men with him swam out to find the scattered crewmen. Some were gasping for breath, having inhaled too many gas fumes. One had an injured leg, and another was in shock. But the one in the worst condition was machinist Patrick McMahon. His face, arms, legs, and feet were covered with hideous burns. Kept afloat only by his life jacket, McMahon had given up all hope. When Kennedy reached him, McMahon was barely conscious.

6   "Go on, skipper," he murmured to Kennedy. "You go on. I've had it."

7   Kennedy ignored McMahon's plea. He grabbed McMahon's life jacket and began towing him back toward what remained of the boat. It was a difficult swim because he was going against a strong current. Also, the bow had already drifted a long way from the men in the water. It took

PT boats played a crucial role in the war in the South Pacific. Many PT boats, like the one in this picture, were camouflaged to blend in with the background of the jungle. These were referred to as "Green Dragons."

Kennedy, who was a strong swimmer, an hour to get McMahon to the bow. During the swim, Kennedy swallowed a lot of seawater mixed with gasoline; this would cause him stomach problems for the rest of his life.

8   At last the 11 survivors were all back on the bow. But they were still far from safe. At any moment the Japanese might spot them and either kill them or take them prisoner. Also, the bow was beginning to take on water. Kennedy knew that in a matter of hours the boat would sink. So on the afternoon of August 2, the men began to swim to a small island about four miles away. (They avoided a closer island because they feared it was occupied by Japanese.) McMahon was still in bad shape; Kennedy had to tow him the entire distance. The other men rigged up a float from the PT's debris. The strong swimmers in the group pushed this makeshift raft through the water with the weaker swimmers tied to it.

9   That night, while the others rested on the island, Kennedy swam out to sea with a small lantern and a pistol. He hoped to flag down another PT boat which could rescue him and his men. He had no luck.

10   On August 4, the men moved to a larger nearby island closer to where PT

boats patrolled. With nothing to eat except coconuts and rainwater, they were all growing weaker. Still, Kennedy again swam with McMahon in tow.

11   The next day Kennedy and another man swam to a third island searching for food. There they found a box with Japanese writing on it. The box contained about 35 small bags of candy and crackers. While on the island, they also saw two men in a canoe. It was clear to Kennedy from their clothing that these men were not enemy soldiers. In fact, they were not enemies at all—they were native islanders. Kennedy tried to hail them, but the islanders didn't see him. Soon they paddled away.

12   Unknown to Kennedy, the two islanders happened to go to the island where the rest of his crew waited. Upon finding the Americans, the islanders offered their help. They gave the men food and even a stove for cooking.

13   When Kennedy returned, he carved a message in the husk of a green coconut and gave it to the islanders. They took the message to a man who could radio for help. This man was a Coastwatcher, one of many scattered throughout the South Pacific during World War II. His job was to hide in the jungle on one of the islands

and report on the movement of enemy ships.

14   At last, on August 8, a PT boat rescued the 11 survivors of *PT 109*. The story made the front page of the *New York Times*. John F. Kennedy became a war hero. For his bravery, the navy awarded him the Navy & Marine Corps Medal. The citation read, in part, "For heroism in the rescue of 3 men following the ramming and sinking of his [PT] boat.... His courage, endurance, and excellent leadership contributed to the saving of several lives." The saga of *PT 109* would later help John F. Kennedy win the 1960 election for president.

If you have been timed while reading this article, enter your reading time below. Then turn to the Words-per-Minute Table on page 133 and look up your reading speed (words per minute). Enter your reading speed on the graph on page 134.

Reading Time: Lesson 14

2 : 52

Minutes   Seconds

A | Finding the Main Idea

One statement below expresses the main idea of the article. One statement is too general, or too broad. The other statement explains only part of the article; it is too narrow. Label the statements using the following key:

M—Main Idea   **B—Too Broad**   **N—Too Narrow**

_____ 1. John Kennedy's PT boat was on duty in the Solomon Islands in the Pacific Ocean during World War II.

_M_ 2. After a Japanese destroyed sank his PT boat, John Kennedy saved the lives of his fellow crew members.

_B_ 3. Sometimes courage and selflessness shown at one time is rewarded later in life.

_____ Score 15 points for a correct M answer.

_____ Score 5 points for each correct B or N answer.

_____ **Total Score:** Finding the Main Idea

B | Recalling Facts

How well do you remember the facts in the article? Put an X in the box next to the answer that correctly completes each statement about the article.

1. PT boats were successful against larger boats because they
   - ☐ a. were small, light, and fast.
   - ☒ b. had better weapons than the larger boats had.
   - ☐ c. had better sailors in command of them.

2. The destroyer instantly killed
   - ☐ a. two crew members.
   - ☒ b. 13 crew members.
   - ☐ c. 25 crew members.

3. Just after the destroyer's attack, Kennedy had the crew
   - ☐ a. try to put out the fires on deck.
   - ☐ b. get into lifeboats.
   - ☒ c. jump into the water.

4. Kennedy towed machinist Patrick McMahon to
   - ☒ a. an island four miles away.
   - ☐ b. the nearest island.
   - ☐ c. a passing U.S. warship.

5. Kennedy wrote an SOS message
   - ☐ a. on the trunk of a tree.
   - ☒ b. in the husk of a coconut.
   - ☐ c. on a slip of paper that he inserted into a bottle.

Score 5 points for each correct answer.

_____ **Total Score:** Recalling Facts

C | Making Inferences

When you combine your own experience and information from a text to draw a conclusion that is not directly stated in that text, you are making an inference. Below are five statements that may or may not be inferences based on information in the article. Label the statements using the following key:

C—Correct Inference   **F—Faulty Inference**

___C___ 1. Kennedy showed concern for his crew throughout the ordeal.

___F___ 2. The fact that the PT boat was surprised so completely meant that their lookout had not been paying attention to his job.

___F___ 3. There are only two islands in the Solomon Island chain.

___C___ 4. The native islanders were sympathetic to the plight of the stranded U.S. sailors.

___C___ 5. Some people may have voted for John Kennedy for president because of the courage he showed as commander of *PT 109*.

Score 5 points for each correct answer.

_____ **Total Score:** Making Inferences

D | Using Words Precisely

Each numbered sentence below contains an underlined word or phrase from the article. Following the sentence are three definitions. One definition is closest to the meaning of the underlined word. One definition is opposite or nearly opposite. Label those two definitions using the following key. Do not label the remaining definition.

C—Closest   **O—Opposite or Nearly Opposite**

1. Their job was to <u>disrupt</u> the Japanese nighttime supply convoys known as the "Tokyo Express."

    ___O___ a. aid

    _____ b. investigate

    ___C___ c. upset or spoil

2. His face, arms, legs, and feet were covered with <u>hideous</u> burns.

    ___C___ a. ugly

    ___O___ b. beautiful

    _____ c. unusual

3. When Kennedy reached him, McMahon was barely <u>conscious</u>.

    ___O___ a. unable to notice surroundings

    _____ b. breathing

    ___C___ c. alert and aware

4. The strong swimmers in the group pushed this <u>makeshift</u> raft through the water with the weaker swimmers tied to it.

    ___C___ a. temporary substitute

    ___O___ b. authentic

    _____ c. ridiculous

5. Kennedy tried to <u>hail</u> them, but the islanders didn't see him.

_____ a. quietly slip by unnoticed

_____ b. annoy

_____ c. get attention by calling out

_____ Score 3 points for each correct C answer.

_____ Score 2 points for each correct O answer.

_____ **Total Score:** Using Words Precisely

Enter the four total scores in the spaces below, and add them together to find your Reading Comprehension Score. Then record your score on the graph on page 135.

Score	Question Type	Lesson 14
_____	Finding the Main Idea	
_____	Recalling Facts	
_____	Making Inferences	
_____	Using Words Precisely	
_____	**Reading Comprehension Score**	

Author's Approach

Put an X in the box next to the correct answer.

1. What is the author's purpose in writing "The Sinking of *PT 109*"?
   ☐ a. To persuade the reader to join the navy
   ☒ b. To inform the reader about a courageous rescue
   ☐ c. To emphasize the differences between PT boats and Japanese destroyers

2. Judging by statements from the article "The Sinking of *PT 109*," you can conclude that the author wants the reader to think that
   ☒ a. Kennedy was a true hero.
   ☐ b. the saga of Kennedy's rescue of his crew has been exaggerated by the press.
   ☐ c. many people think that Kennedy made the wrong decision when he had the men jump into the water after the destroyer struck.

3. How is the author's purpose for writing the article expressed in paragraph 7?
   ☐ a. The paragraph points out that Kennedy refused to pay attention to McMahon's pleas.
   ☐ b. The paragraph mentions that Kennedy was a strong swimmer.
   ☒ c. The paragraph points out that Kennedy rescued his fellow crew member at great cost to his own health.

4. The author tells this story mainly by
   ☒ a. describing events in the order they happened.
   ☐ b. comparing different topics.
   ☐ c. using his or her imagination and creativity.

_____ Number of correct answers

Record your personal assessment of your work on the Critical Thinking Chart on page 136.

Summarizing and Paraphrasing

Put an X in the box next to the correct answer.

1. Below are summaries of the article. Choose the summary that says all the most important things about the article but in the fewest words.

☐ a. John Kennedy's reputation as an authentic American hero began with an incident during World War II, when Kennedy was commander of the *PT 109*.

☐ b. A Japanese destroyer surprised the *PT 109* on August 2, 1943, and torpedoed the little boat, commanded by John Kennedy. First, Kennedy ordered the surviving members of the crew to jump into the water because he was afraid that the boat would blow up. But later, the whole crew swam to an island four miles away.

☒ c. When a Japanese destroyer torpedoed *PT 109*, commanded by John Kennedy, Kennedy led his crew to safety; his courage earned him a medal and later helped him win the presidency.

2. Choose the sentence that correctly restates the following sentence from the article:

"Instead, they [the PT boats] had to attack at night, like mosquitoes, and then quickly dash for cover behind one of the many islands in the region."

☐ a. There were plenty of mosquitoes on the islands in the region, near which the PT boats patrolled.

☒ b. Like annoying stinging insects, the PT boats attacked only at night and then quickly hid behind one of the nearby islands.

☐ c. The PT boats were able to perform well only because they were near mosquito-filled islands behind which they could hide.

_____ Number of correct answers

Record your personal assessment of your work on the Critical Thinking Chart on page 136.

Critical Thinking

Follow the directions provided for questions 1, 2, and 3. Put an X in the box next to the correct answer for the other questions.

1. For each statement below, write O if it expresses an opinion or write F if it expresses a fact.

___F___ a. The navy awarded Kennedy the Navy & Marine Corps Medal for heroism.

___O___ b. Kennedy was the bravest man in the entire *PT 109* crew.

___F___ c. At 2:30 in the morning on August 2, 1943, the *PT 109* was torpedoed by a Japanese destroyer.

2. Choose from the letters below to correctly complete the following statement. Write the letters on the lines.

On the positive side, ___b___, but on the negative side ___c___.

a. Kennedy led the men to an island about four miles away

b. Kennedy's actions saved many lives

c. Kennedy suffered from stomach troubles for the rest of his life because he swallowed seawater mixed with gasoline

3. Read paragraph 10. Then choose from the letters below to correctly complete the following statement. Write the letters on the lines.

According to paragraph 10, ___a___ because ___c___.

a. the men were grower weaker

b. Kennedy towed McMahon to a larger island

c. the men had nothing to eat except coconuts and rainwater

4. How is "The Sinking of *PT 109*" related to the theme of *Rescued*?

☐ a. It describes the activities of the navy in the Pacific during World War II.

☑ b. It tells how John Kennedy contributed to the saving of several lives.

☐ c. It explains how John Kennedy became president of the United States.

5. What did you have to do to answer question 1?

☐ a. find an opinion (what someone thinks about something)

☐ b. find a description (how something looks)

☑ c. draw a conclusion (a sensible statement based on the text and your experience)

_____ Number of correct answers

Record your personal assessment of your work on the Critical Thinking Chart on page 136.

Personal Response

Why do you think John Kennedy risked his own life to save Patrick McMahon?

_____

_____

_____

Self-Assessment

When reading the article, I was having trouble with

_____

_____

_____

_____

_____

_____

Compare and Contrast

Think about the articles you have read in Unit Two. Pick four rescues that you feel were the most difficult. Write the titles of the articles in the first column of the chart below. Use information you learned from the articles to fill in the empty boxes in the chart.

Title	What difficulties did the rescuer overcome?	What physical or mental qualities did the rescuer need?	What dangers did the rescuer put himself or herself into?

If I could take part in any of these rescues, I would choose _____ because _____

_____

_____

Words-per-Minute Table

Unit Two

Directions: If you were timed while reading an article, refer to the Reading Time you recorded in the box at the end of the article. Use this words-per-minute table to determine your reading speed for that article. Then plot your reading speed on the graph on page 134.

Lesson No. of Words	8 845	9 1135	10 944	11 1071	12 1362	13 1007	14 1117	Seconds
1:30	563	757	629	715	908	671	745	90
1:40	507	681	566	643	817	604	670	100
1:50	461	619	515	585	743	549	609	110
2:00	423	568	472	536	681	504	559	120
2:10	390	524	436	495	629	465	516	130
2:20	362	486	405	459	584	432	479	140
2:30	338	454	378	429	545	403	447	150
2:40	317	426	354	402	511	378	419	160
2:50	298	401	333	378	481	355	394	170
3:00	282	378	315	357	454	336	372	180
3:10	267	358	298	339	430	318	353	190
3:20	254	341	283	322	409	302	335	200
3:30	241	324	270	306	389	288	319	210
3:40	230	310	257	292	371	275	305	220
3:50	220	296	246	280	355	263	291	230
4:00	211	284	236	268	341	252	279	240
4:10	203	272	227	257	327	242	268	250
4:20	195	262	218	247	314	232	258	260
4:30	188	252	210	238	303	224	248	270
4:40	181	243	202	230	292	216	239	280
4:50	175	235	195	222	282	208	231	290
5:00	169	227	189	214	272	201	223	300
5:10	164	220	183	207	264	195	216	310
5:20	158	213	177	201	255	189	209	320
5:30	154	206	172	195	248	183	203	330
5:40	149	200	167	189	240	178	197	340
5:50	145	195	162	184	233	173	191	350
6:00	141	189	157	179	227	168	186	360
6:10	137	184	153	174	221	163	181	370
6:20	133	179	149	169	215	159	176	380
6:30	130	175	145	165	210	155	172	390
6:40	127	170	142	161	204	151	168	400
6:50	124	166	138	157	199	147	163	410
7:00	121	162	135	153	195	144	160	420
7:10	118	158	132	150	190	141	156	430
7:20	115	155	129	146	186	137	152	440
7:30	113	151	126	143	182	134	149	450
7:40	110	148	123	140	178	131	146	460
7:50	108	145	121	137	174	129	143	470
8:00	106	142	118	134	170	126	140	480

Minutes and Seconds

Plotting Your Progress: Reading Speed

Unit Two

Directions: If you were timed while reading an article, write your words-per-minute rate for that article in the box under the number of the lesson. Then plot your reading speed on the graph by putting a small X on the line directly above the number of the lesson, across from the number of words per minute you read. As you mark your speed for each lesson, graph your progress by drawing a line to connect the X's.

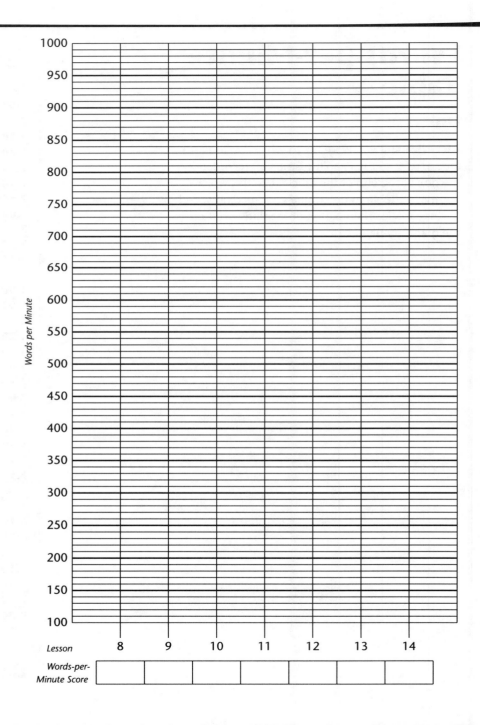

Words per Minute

Lesson 8 9 10 11 12 13 14

Words-per-Minute Score

Plotting Your Progress: Reading Comprehension

Unit Two

Directions: Write your Reading Comprehension score for each lesson in the box under the number of the lesson. Then plot your score on the graph by putting a small X on the line directly above the number of the lesson and across from the score you earned. As you mark your score for each lesson, graph your progress by drawing a line to connect the X's.

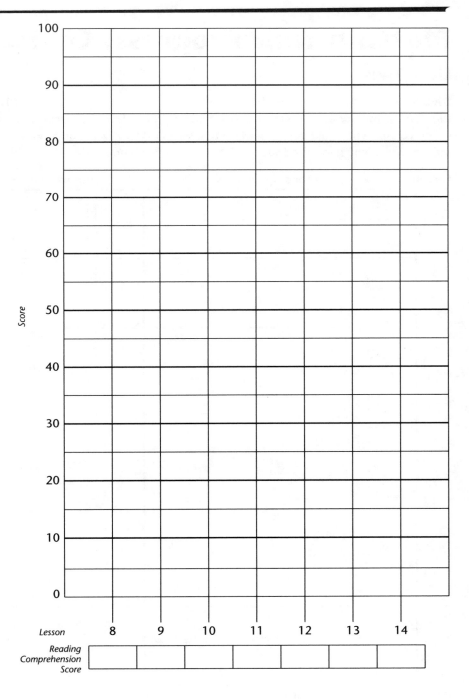

Plotting Your Progress: Critical Thinking

Unit Two

Directions: Work with your teacher to evaluate your responses to the Critical Thinking questions for each lesson. Then fill in the appropriate spaces in the chart below. For each lesson and each type of Critical Thinking question, do the following: Mark a minus sign (–) in the box to indicate areas in which you feel you could improve. Mark a plus sign (+) to indicate areas in which you feel you did well. Mark a minus-slash-plus sign (–/+) to indicate areas in which you had mixed success. Then write any comments you have about your performance, including ideas for improvement.

Lesson	Author's Approach	Summarizing and Paraphrasing	Critical Thinking
8			
9			
10			
11			
12			
13			
14			

UNIT THREE

"SUPERMAN" TO THE RESCUE

Anytime you jump out of an airplane, you take a calculated risk. In a skydiver's famous spread-eagle position, you're falling at about 120 miles per hour. Once you open your parachute, however, you slow down and float gently to the ground at no more than 10 miles per hour. So, in truth, the odds of surviving are in your favor. Many skydivers make hundreds of jumps without suffering so much as a twisted knee or a sprained ankle.

2   But successful jumps are almost never the ones that you read about in the newspaper. It's the rare exception that usually captures everyone's attention. Such a jump took place at Coolidge, Arizona, on April 18, 1987. Skydivers from all over the country had come to enjoy an Easter weekend of parachuting. One of the jumps was a near disaster, but thanks to the heroics of Gregory "Superman" Robertson, no one was killed.

3   Experienced skydivers look for new challenges, new ways to test their skill. One way of doing that is by creating formations, such as the "six-way" circle, while falling through the air. In the "six-way" routine, four jumpers go out of the plane first and quickly form a horizontal circle by holding hands. Then a fifth jumper dives down to join them. He or she must travel faster than 120 miles per hour in order the catch the first four. To

move that fast, the jumper tucks in his or her body a little bit to gain speed. Finally, a sixth jumper dives down to complete the six-way. This jumper, of course, has the hardest job because he or she has to dive even faster than the fifth jumper to link up in the circle. Once joined, all the jumpers hold the circle until they are ready to open their parachutes. Then they separate and—if all goes well—land safely. When it goes as planned, the six-way is a very pretty sight.

4   Debbie Williams, a fifth grade teacher, was eager to do a six-way jump. On April 17, she and five others made two successful six-ways. The next morning they

executed another six-way jump without a hitch, and planned to do a final one that afternoon. Back in the hanger, however, Williams was having trouble with her chute. (Most skydivers pack their own chutes after each jump so they have no one to blame but themselves if the chute doesn't open.) Safety adviser Gregory Robertson saw Williams struggling with the snarled lines. "How many jumps have you made?" Robertson asked after introducing himself.

5   "Fifty-five," she answered.

6   To most people—especially those who would never consider jumping out of a plane—that figure might sound high. But

This group of skydivers forms circles as they free fall. The landscape below provides an indication of how high they are above the ground.

Gregory Robertson dove at a speed of about 180 miles per hour to save the unconscious Debbie Williams.

to Robertson, who had completed over 1,700 jumps, the number meant that Williams did not have much experience. So he decided to keep an eye on her.

7   When afternoon came, Williams climbed into the four-engine DC-4 jump plane along with 90 other parachutists. Gregory Robertson was on board to assist them. After the plane reached about 13,500 feet, Robertson began to send groups of skydivers on their way. Williams and her group were the last to jump, followed closely by Robertson himself. As Williams and her partners gathered at the door, they all shouted in agreement, "Six-way!" But it surprised Robertson that Williams would be the sixth jumper. With her relative lack of experience, he thought she should have been one of the first four.

8   Things went wrong right from the beginning. Guy Fitzwater, one of the first four jumpers, became caught in a back-wash from the plane and was pulled away from the others. That left a base circle with only three jumpers. Fitzwater tried to dive back into the formation but missed. As he slowed down to try again, Alex Rodriquez, the fifth jumper, joined the circle, but he came in so fast that he tilted the circle from a horizontal position to a vertical one.

9   This was a highly dangerous situation. For starters, the jumpers in the circle were now going faster than planned. In addition, the jumpers were stacked up vertically, with Fitzwater and Williams only a few hundred feet above them. The lower jumpers needed to open their chutes soon, but if they did so, the skydivers

above would have little time to react. If the skydivers hit an open chute, the collision would collapse the chute, causing a fatal fall.

10   Robertson saw all this and moved in to steer Williams away from the danger. But before he could get there, both Williams and Fitzwater went into a dive to catch up to the circle. Williams used a body position that caused her to go much faster than Fitzwater, but her angle was off. She smashed into Fitzwater's backpack with so much force that the blow knocked her unconscious. Now she began to tumble like a rag doll.

11   Robertson watched in horror from above. In an instant, he decided that Fitzwater, although injured, seemed well enough to land without assistance. In any event, there was no way Robertson could save both jumpers. He quickly positioned his body to go into the steepest dive possible, hoping to catch Williams before it was too late to open her chute. By pinning his arms to his side, tucking his head to his chest, and crossing his ankles, he became a vertical dart. Soon he was speeding straight down at 180 miles per hour.

12   As he cut through the air, Robertson managed to steal a glance at Williams and, using subtle shoulder movements, zeroed in on her. At about 3,500 feet, he caught up with her and opened up his body to slow down to Williams's speed. The two jumpers were just seconds away from impact. At last, at 2,000 feet, Robertson pulled the rip cord on Williams's para-chute. Then he pulled his own rip cord.

13   The parachutes opened in the nick of time. Because Debbie Williams was uncon-scious, however, she could not position herself to land without injury. Fortunately, she landed on her back and not her neck, which might have killed her. Still, she was badly hurt. Medics rushed her by heli-copter to the hospital. Her injuries were extensive: a skull fracture, broken ribs, a bruised kidney, a bruised lung, and a lac-erated liver. She remained on the critical list for nine days, but ultimately made a full recovery.

14   Only one other skydiver had ever pulled off such a daring rescue. The other times it had been tried, both jumpers ended up dead. Still, Gregory Robertson, who was dubbed "Superman" by the media, did not see himself as a hero. His entry in his logbook reflected this modest view: "Pulled unconscious girl's rip cord. We both lived."

If you have been timed while reading this article, enter your reading time below. Then turn to the Words-per-Minute Table on page 195 and look up your reading speed (words per minute). Enter your reading speed on the graph on page 196.

Reading Time: Lesson 15

<u>   4   </u> : <u>   O9   </u>
Minutes   *Seconds*

A | Finding the Main Idea

One statement below expresses the main idea of the article. One statement is too general, or too broad. The other statement explains only part of the article; it is too narrow. Label the statements using the following key:

M—Main Idea   **B—Too Broad**   **N—Too Narrow**

_N_ 1. Skydiver Debbie Williams had made 55 jumps before she stepped out of the plane on April 18, 1987.

_B_ 2. Skydiving can be a dangerous sport.

_M_ 3. One skydiver's life had been put into danger by a series of unfortunate accidents, but another fast-thinking skydiver saved her from certain death.

_____ Score 15 points for a correct M answer.

_____ Score 5 points for each correct B or N answer.

_____ **Total Score:** Finding the Main Idea

B | Recalling Facts

How well do you remember the facts in the article? Put an X in the box next to the answer that correctly completes each statement about the article.

1. In the spread-eagle position, skydivers fall at a speed of
   - ☐ a. 75 miles per hour.
   - ☐ b. 100 miles per hour.
   - ☒ c. 120 miles per hour.

2. In the usual six-way formation, a horizontal circle is first made by
   - ☐ a. three skydivers holding hands.
   - ☒ b. four skydivers holding hands.
   - ☐ c. six skydivers holding hands.

3. Gregory Robertson had completed about
   - ☐ a. 500 jumps.
   - ☐ b. 120 jumps.
   - ☒ c. 1,700 jumps.

4. Debbie Williams was knocked unconscious when she
   - ☒ a. bumped into Fitzwater's backpack.
   - ☐ b. hit her head on the plane.
   - ☐ c. hit the ground.

5. Williams finally landed on her
   - ☐ a. neck.
   - ☒ b. back.
   - ☐ c. feet.

Score 5 points for each correct answer.

_____ **Total Score:** Recalling Facts

C | Making Inferences

When you combine your own experience and information from a text to draw a conclusion that is not directly stated in that text, you are making an inference. Below are five statements that may or may not be inferences based on information in the article. Label the statements using the following key:

C—Correct Inference   F—Faulty Inference

_C_ 1. Completing skydiving formations takes more skill than individual skydiving requires.

_F_ 2. Only very experienced skydivers are allowed to try the six-way formation.

_C_ 3. Williams packed her parachute improperly.

_C_ 4. Without Gregory Robertson's quick action, Debbie Williams would most likely have been killed.

_C_ 5. Debbie Williams had jumped with the same group of skydivers many times before the Easter weekend at Coolidge.

Score 5 points for each correct answer.

_____ **Total Score:** Making Inferences

D | Using Words Precisely

Each numbered sentence below contains an underlined word or phrase from the article. Following the sentence are three definitions. One definition is closest to the meaning of the underlined word. One definition is opposite or nearly opposite. Label those two definitions using the following key. Do not label the remaining definition.

C—Closest   O—Opposite or Nearly Opposite

1. The next morning they <u>executed</u> another "six-way" jump….

   _O_ a. failed to do

   _C_ b. accomplished

   ____ c. read about

2. Safety adviser Gregory Robertson saw Williams struggling with the <u>snarled</u> lines.

   _O_ a. straight and organized

   ____ b. heavy

   _C_ c. tangled

3. …Robertson managed to steal a glance at Williams and, using <u>subtle</u> shoulder movements, zeroed in on her.

   _O_ a. exaggerated

   _C_ b. delicate and slight

   ____ c. useless

4. Her injuries were <u>extensive</u>: a skull fracture, broken ribs, a bruised kidney, a bruised lung, and a lacerated liver.

   ____ a. pitiful

   _O_ b. slight and extremely limited

   _C_ c. considerable and wide-spread

5. His entry in his logbook reflected this <u>modest</u> view: "Pulled unconscious girl's rip cord. We both lived."

_____ a. out-of-date

_____ b. humble

_____ c. boastful

_____ Score 3 points for each correct C answer.

_____ Score 2 points for each correct O answer.

_____ **Total Score:** Using Words Precisely

Enter the four total scores in the spaces below, and add them together to find your Reading Comprehension Score. Then record your score on the graph on page 197.

Score	Question Type	Lesson 15
_____	Finding the Main Idea	
_____	Recalling Facts	
_____	Making Inferences	
_____	Using Words Precisely	
_____	**Reading Comprehension Score**	

Author's Approach

Put an X in the box next to the correct answer.

1. The author uses the first sentence of the article to
   a. introduce the topic of the article.
   b. explain why people skydive.
   c. compare skydiving and stunt flying.

2. What does the author imply by saying "But it surprised Robertson that Williams would be the sixth jumper. With her relative lack of experience, he thought she should have been one of the first four"?
   a. Robertson was totally in charge of the skydivers' activities.
   b. Robertson and the skydivers had thoroughly discussed the role of each skydiver before the plane left the ground.
   c. Robertson had no control over the skydivers' plans.

3. Choose the statement below that best describes the author's position in paragraph 2.
   a. Coolidge, Arizona, is a good place for skydiving.
   b. Gregory Robertson acted like a hero, making sure no one was killed while skydiving.
   c. The Easter weekend of parachuting held at Coolidge, Arizona, was not properly managed.

_____ Number of correct answers

Record your personal assessment of your work on the Critical Thinking Chart on page 198.

Summarizing and Paraphrasing

Follow the directions provided for question 1. Put an X in the box next to the correct answer for question 2.

1. Look for the important ideas and events in paragraphs 13 and 14. Summarize those paragraphs in one or two sentences.

_____

_____

_____

2. Read the statement about the article below. Then read the paraphrase of that statement. Choose the reason that best tells why the paraphrase does not say the same thing as the statement.

   Statement: When Rodriquez tried to join the circle of skydivers, he came in so fast that he tilted the circle vertically instead of horizontally.

   Paraphrase: Rodriquez changed the circle's tilt when he tried to join the other skydivers.

   ☐ a.   Paraphrase says too much.

   ☒ b.   Paraphrase doesn't say enough.

   ☐ c.   Paraphrase doesn't agree with the statement about the article.

_____ Number of correct answers

Record your personal assessment of your work on the Critical Thinking Chart on page 198.

Critical Thinking

Put an X in the box next to the correct answer for questions 1, 3, and 4. Follow the directions provided for the other questions.

1. Considering Gregory Robertson's actions as described in this article, you can predict that

   ☒ a.   Debbie Williams will always be grateful to him.

   ☐ b.   he will never skydive again.

   ☐ c.   the next time he has a chance to save someone's life, he will think of his own safety first.

2. Using what you know about Gregory Robertson and what is told about Debbie Williams in the article, name three ways Robertson is similar to and three ways Robertson is different from Williams. Cite the paragraph number(s) where you found details in the article to support your conclusions.

   Similarities

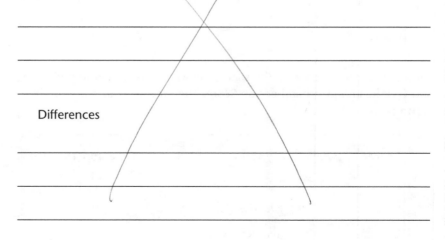

   _____

   _____

   _____

   Differences

   _____

   _____

   _____

3. What was the effect of Debbie Williams's incorrect angle when she tried to catch up with the circle?

☞ a. Williams ran into Fitzwater's backpack.

☐ b. Williams knocked the circle vertical.

☐ c. Williams missed the circle altogether.

4. If you were a safety adviser for skydivers, how could you use the information in the article to increase the skydivers' chances of success while still allowing them to have fun?

☞ a. You could demand that the fifth and sixth jumpers in a six-way be very experienced skydivers.

☞ b. You could forbid anyone from trying difficult stunts.

☞ c. You could be ready to help in case of emergencies.

5. In which paragraph did you find your information or details to answer question 3?

_____

_____ Number of correct answers

Record your personal assessment of your work on the Critical Thinking Chart on page 198.

Personal Response

I know the feeling that Gregory Robertson had when he saw everything going wrong because

_____

_____

_____

_____

Self-Assessment

I'm proud of how I answered question # _____ in section _____ because

_____

_____

_____

_____

BENEATH THE RUBBLE

In California, people live in fear of the Big One—a massive earthquake along the San Andreas fault that will take thousands, if not tens of thousands, of lives. While they are waiting for the Big One, however, Californians have experienced plenty of Small Ones. Even these small earthquakes have managed to decimate whole regions.

2   On January 17, 1994, a "small" earthquake, showing 6.8 on the Richter scale, hit Northridge, California. (The Richter scale is used to measure the ground motion during an earthquake. The largest recorded quake hit Japan in 1933. It measured 8.9 on the Richter scale.) The Northridge quake lasted just 30 seconds. It hit in the early morning, when most people were in bed sleeping. At 4:30 A.M. all was peaceful and quiet. Less than a minute later, however, the region around Northridge, a suburb of Los Angeles, looked as if it had just been bombed. Highways had ruptured and split in two. Downed power lines had plunged more than three million people into darkness. Broken gas and oil lines caused countless fires. And a total of 61 people died during

A condominium building sits on most of a car after collapsing during the earthquake that hit Northridge, California, in 1994.

the quake or later as a result of injuries caused by the quake.

3   It was in the wake of this disaster that a heroic rescue took place. The rescue centered around Salvador Pena, who had left his native El Salvador 12 years earlier to escape a civil war and start a new life in the United States. Pena worked two jobs to support his wife and five children. During the day, he worked as a janitor at a local college, and at night he ran a street sweeper at the Northridge Fashion Plaza.

4   At 4:30 A.M. on January 17, Pena was driving his power sweeper on the lower level of the mall's three-story parking garage. When the earthquake struck, the garage began to shake violently, and Pena realized that he had no time to escape. "It happened so fast, I wasn't able to do anything," he said later. "I put myself in God's hands." Within seconds, the parking garage crumbled like a house of cards, trapping Pena—still inside his sweeper—beneath 20 tons of concrete.

5   The search for survivors began right away. Firefighters and paramedics soon found Pena, but then faced the monumental task of getting him out. Rescuers managed to dig a passageway to him, but this tunnel was unstable at best and was studded with chunks of concrete and twisted ribbons of metal. When firefighter Vincent Jenkins crawled

through it the first time, he could see only Pena's upper body. As the rescue work proceeded, Jenkins crawled through the tunnel again and again, bringing encouragement and comfort to the trapped man.

This collapsed roadway was a result of the Northridge earthquake.

Pena, for his part, never lost consciousness or his faith in God. At one point he even asked his rescuers to pray with him. Although he feared death was near, Pena later said he refused to give up the struggle to live because he felt that his family would not survive without his support. "I've always fought to give them food," he said, "give them a little strength to sustain themselves."

6 The rescuers couldn't just pull Pena out because his legs were pinned beneath the rubble. They had to use jackhammers to clear away the loose debris in the tunnel, and then they had to drill holes into the concrete that was resting on top of the sweeper. These holes allowed the paramedics to pump oxygen in to Pena. The holes also allowed the rescuers to slip four plastic air bags into the space around Pena. Then rescuers inflated the bags, lifting the concrete off Pena's legs. To get him out of the sweeper, the rescuers had to cut off the roof of the vehicle, its door, and its entire dashboard. Only then could the rescuers free him. "He was pinned between two beams," said Jenkins, "and they had to lift in unison to free him."

7 The whole rescue was covered on television, and a large crowd had gathered at the site. Everyone cheered when, after eight hours, Salvador Pena at last appeared on a stretcher from beneath the rubble. His body was broken and bloodied, but he was still alive. Pena was quickly placed on a rescue helicopter and rushed to the UCLA Medical Center.

8 But Pena was not out of danger yet. He had suffered a partially dislocated spine. Also, doctors feared that they might have to amputate his crushed right hand, as well as both his legs. Five surgeons labored for five hours on Pena's injured limbs, making almost a dozen inch incisions to relieve swelling and reduce pressure. Luckily, they were successful and Pena was soon on the mend.

9 Despite his painful ordeal, Pena remained optimistic, even sunny, as his body healed. He poured out praise for the many people who had played a role in saving his life. Doctor Michael J. Zinner said, "He's just remarkable—bright and responsive. He's a wonderfully courageous man who is extremely lucky to be alive."

10 In another sense, the whole Northridge region was lucky. The earthquake happened so early in the day that most people were home rather than in vulnerable places such as the Northridge Fashion Plaza. "If this had happened during daylight hours," said Doctor Zinner, "there would have been hundreds of Mr. Penas and not much we could do for them." And keep in mind, the Northridge earthquake was just a "Small One." What if the next earthquake to strike is the Big One? 🌿

If you have been timed while reading this article, enter your reading time below. Then turn to the Words-per-Minute Table on page 195 and look up your reading speed (words per minute). Enter your reading speed on the graph on page 196.

Reading Time: Lesson 16

2 : 29

Minutes   Seconds

A | Finding the Main Idea

One statement below expresses the main idea of the article. One statement is too general, or too broad. The other statement explains only part of the article; it is too narrow. Label the statements using the following key:

M—Main Idea   **B—Too Broad**   **N—Too Narrow**

 1. Showing persistence and courage, workers rescued a man who had been pinned under the rubble of an earthquake in Northridge, California.

2. When an earthquake strikes, the efficiency of emergency crews are put to the test.

3. Salvador Pena was running a street sweeper in the parking garage of the Northridge Fashion Plaza when an earthquake that measured 6.8 on the Richter scale struck.

_____ Score 15 points for a correct M answer.

_____ Score 5 points for each correct B or N answer.

_____ **Total Score:** Finding the Main Idea

B | Recalling Facts

How well do you remember the facts in the article? Put an X in the box next to the answer that correctly completes each statement about the article.

1. Northridge is a suburb of
   - ☒ a. Los Angeles.
   - ☐ b. San Francisco.
   - ☐ c. San Diego.

2. Salvador Pena moved to the United States from
   - ☐ a. Guatemala.
   - ☒ b. El Salvador.
   - ☐ c. Mexico.

3. The earthquake struck at
   - ☒ a. 4:30 P.M.
   - ☐ b. 1:00 P.M.
   - ☒ c. 4:30 A.M.

4. Pena's rescue took
   - ☐ a. one hour.
   - ☒ b. eight hours.
   - ☐ c. 24 hours.

5. Pena suffered all these injuries except a
   - ☒ a. fractured skull.
   - ☐ b. dislocated spine.
   - ☐ c. crushed hand.

Score 5 points for each correct answer.

_____ **Total Score:** Recalling Facts

C | Making Inferences

When you combine your own experience and information from a text to draw a conclusion that is not directly stated in that text, you are making an inference. Below are five statements that may or may not be inferences based on information in the article. Label the statements using the following key:

C—Correct Inference   **F—Faulty Inference**

_____ C   1. At first, most residents of Northridge thought that a bomb, not an earthquake, had struck their city.

_____ C   2. Most people feel happy and relieved when someone, even a stranger, is rescued.

_____ C   3. All the television stations in the Los Angeles area suffered long-lasting power failures as a result of the earthquake.

_____ C   4. If an earthquake measuring more than 6.8 on the Richter scale hit the Los Angeles area, it would do even more damage than this quake did.

_____ F   5. Maintenance workers in shopping malls often do their jobs before and after regular working hours.

Score 5 points for each correct answer.

_____ **Total Score:** Making Inferences

D | Using Words Precisely

Each numbered sentence below contains an underlined word or phrase from the article. Following the sentence are three definitions. One definition is closest to the meaning of the underlined word. One definition is opposite or nearly opposite. Label those two definitions using the following key. Do not label the remaining definition.

C—Closest   **O—Opposite or Nearly Opposite**

1. Even these small earthquakes have managed to <u>decimate</u> whole regions.

_____   a. surprise

_____ O   b. rebuild

_____ C   c. destroy

2. Firefighters and paramedics soon found Pena, but then faced the <u>monumental</u> task of getting him out.

_____   a. annoying

_____ C   b. huge and overwhelming

_____ O   c. insignificant

3. "He was pinned between two beams," said Jenkins, "and they had to lift <u>in unison</u> to free him."

_____ C   a. all together

_____   b. energetically

_____ O   c. one after the other

4. Despite his painful ordeal, Pena remained <u>optimistic</u>, even sunny, as his body healed.

_____ O   a. always depressed

_____   b. childlike

_____ C   c. habitually cheerful

5. The earthquake happened so early in the day that most people were home rather than in <u>vulnerable</u> places such as the Northridge Fashion Plaza.

_____ *C* a. unprotected

_____ b. popular

_____ *O* c. safe

_____ Score 3 points for each correct C answer.

_____ Score 2 points for each correct O answer.

_____ **Total Score:** Using Words Precisely

Enter the four total scores in the spaces below, and add them together to find your Reading Comprehension Score. Then record your score on the graph on page 197.

Score	Question Type	Lesson 16
_____	Finding the Main Idea	
_____	Recalling Facts	
_____	Making Inferences	
_____	Using Words Precisely	
_____	**Reading Comprehension Score**	

Author's Approach

Put an X in the box next to the correct answer.

1. What does the author mean by the statement "'If this [the earthquake] had happened during daylight hours,' said Doctor Zinner, 'there would have been hundreds of Mr. Penas and not much we could do for them'"?

☐ a. If the quake hadn't happened at night, Mr. Pena could not have been rescued.

☒ b. If the quake had happened during regular daytime business hours, many more people would have needed to be rescued.

☐ c. Emergency crews do not work during daylight hours, so if the quake had happened then, many people would not have been rescued in time.

2. Which of the following statements from the article best describes Salvador Pena's state of mind during his ordeal?

☐ a. "But Pena was not out of danger yet. He had suffered a partially dislocated spine."

☒ b. "Pena, for his part, never lost consciousness or his faith in God."

☐ c. "During the day, he worked as a janitor at a local college, and at night he ran a street sweeper at the Northridge Fashion Plaza."

3. From the statements below, choose those that you believe the author would agree with.

☐ a. California is the only place in the world where residents are concerned about possible earthquakes.

☐ b. Californians are needlessly worried about big earthquakes.

☒ c. Many people believe that someday a really big earthquake will hit California.

4. Judging by statements from the article "Beneath the Rubble," you can conclude that the author wants the reader to think that

☐ a.   If you met Salvador Pena, you probably wouldn't like him.

☒ b.   Salvador Pena would make a good friend.

☐ c.   Salvador Pena complains a great deal.

_____ Number of correct answers

Record your personal assessment of your work on the Critical Thinking Chart on page 198.

Summarizing and Paraphrasing

Follow the directions provided for question 1. Put an X in the box next to the correct answer for the other questions.

1. Reread paragraph 4 in the article. Below, write a summary of the paragraph in no more than 25 words.

Earthquake hits

_____

_____

Reread your summary and decide whether it covers the important ideas in the paragraph. Next, decide how to shorten the summary to 15 words or less without leaving out any essential information. Write this summary below.

_____

_____

2. Read the statement about the article below. Then read the paraphrase of that statement. Choose the reason that best tells why the paraphrase does not say the same thing as the statement.

Statement: Although he suffered many injuries, Salvador Pena refused to give up, saying that his family needed him.

Paraphrase: Salvador Pena refused to give up.

☐ a.   Paraphrase says too much.

☒ b.   Paraphrase doesn't say enough.

☐ c.   Paraphrase doesn't agree with the statement about the article.

3. Choose the best one-sentence paraphrase for the following sentence from the article:
"Downed power lines had plunged more than three million people into darkness."

☐ a.   More than three million people reported that the downed power lines created a strange darkness on the day of the earthquake.

☒ b.   More than three million people were affected by a power outage caused by downed power lines.

☐ c.   More than three million people could not see the downed power lines because of the darkness.

_____ Number of correct answers

Record your personal assessment of your work on the Critical Thinking Chart on page 198.

Critical Thinking

Put an X in the box next to the correct answer for questions 1, 3, and 4. Follow the directions provided for question 2.

1. Which of the following statements from the article is an opinion rather than a fact?

☐ a. "Pena was quickly placed on a rescue helicopter and rushed to the UCLA Medical Center."

☒ b. "…'He's a wonderfully courageous man who is extremely lucky to be alive.'"

☐ c. "The whole rescue was covered on television, and a large crowd had gathered at the site."

2. Think about cause-effect relationships in the article. Fill in the blanks in the cause-effect chart, drawing from the letters below.

Cause	Effect
The earthquake hit Northridge.	_____ C
Pena's legs were pinned under rubble.	_____ A
_____ b	Rescuers were able to pump oxygen to Pena.

a. Rescuers couldn't simply pull Pena out.

b. Rescuers drilled holes into the concrete on top of Pena's sweeper.

c. The Northridge Fashion Plaza garage crumbled.

3. How is "Beneath the Rubble" related to the theme of this book?

☒ a. A group of emergency workers saved Salvador Pena from being crushed under rubble.

☐ b. An earthquake killed 61 people in the Northridge, California, area.

☐ c. Salvador Pena never lost his faith in God throughout his ordeal.

4. What did you have to do to answer question 1?

☒ a. find a reason (why something is the way it is)

☐ b. find an opinion (what someone thinks about something)

☒ c. draw a conclusion (a sensible statement based on the text and your experience)

_____ Number of correct answers

Record your personal assessment of your work on the Critical Thinking Chart on page 198.

Personal Response

Begin the first 5–8 sentences of your own article about being caught in an earthquake. It may tell of a real experience or one that is imagined.

_____

_____

_____

_____

Self-Assessment

I was confused on question # _____ in section _____ because

_____

_____

_____

SHOT DOWN BEHIND ENEMY LINES

In February 1991, Captain Scott O'Grady found himself alone, cold, and hungry in the mountains of Washington state. He had to eat black ants and grasshoppers in order to survive. He had to start fires using the rays of the sun and make tools out of tree branches. And to ward off boredom, he played "entire rounds of golf and chess" in his mind. Yes, it was a brutal and grueling test for O'Grady, but it was only a test. The jet pilot was taking the U.S. Air Force's three-week Survival, Evasion, Resistance, and Escape (SERE) course just in case he ever needed these skills.

2   He did. On June 2, 1995, Captain O'Grady took off in his F-16 jet fighter for a routine air patrol over Bosnia. On this mission, Captain Bob Wright flew alongside in a second F-16. Both pilots were part of a multinational military force trying to stop Serbian attacks in Bosnia.

3   As O'Grady and Wright flew their patrol, the Serbs launched two surface-to-air missiles at the two F-16s. O'Grady's instruments picked up the incoming missiles, but he could not see them because the sky was cloudy. One missile exploded in the air, doing no harm to

Captain Scott O'Grady flew an F-16 similar to this one in his air patrol over Bosnia in 1995.

either plane, but the second missile sheared O'Grady's jet in half. As the front section of the jet tumbled toward the ground, O'Grady pulled a special cord that blew away his canopy and ejected him from the cockpit. He then parachuted into the Serb-held hills of western Bosnia.

4   Right after landing, O'Grady got rid of his parachute and dashed into the woods, hoping to avoid capture. He fell face down on the ground and covered his head and ears with his camouflaged gloves to make himself harder to see. Civilians and soldiers were all around. Once O'Grady saw armed soldiers walking nearby. He whispered a silent prayer of thanks that they did *not* have sniffing dogs.

5   Now O'Grady really needed the training he had received in the SERE course. He had the necessary equipment to evade the enemy and to survive for several days—a radio, a compass, flares, a first-aid kit, a knife, a pistol, and other such items. And the SERE course had taught him how to live off the land. He used a sponge to soak up rainwater, and he ate grass, bugs, and grasshoppers. He slept during the day, hidden under a camouflaged cover, and traveled only after midnight.

6   O'Grady didn't use his radio to call for help right away. His training had taught him that downed pilots are often captured because they radio too soon, giving away

their position. So he watched and waited for the right time. After five and a half days, O'Grady finally took a chance and at 2:08 A.M. on June 8, broadcast his call sign: "Basher 52." His voice was picked up by a patrolling F-16 jet. This was the first time anyone actually knew that O'Grady had survived the missile attack and was still alive. Captain Wright had last seen him going down through the clouds and hadn't seen his parachute open.

A soldier patrols the front lines in Sarajevo.

7 A rescue operation had already been planned just in case O'Grady was still alive. It was a huge effort involving 40 aircraft, a half-dozen ships, and more than 100 soldiers. There was a primary team as well as backup teams—all willing to risk their lives to save the downed pilot. As it turned out, the backup teams were not needed because the primary team did its job so well.

8 At 5:50 A.M., less than three hours after O'Grady's message was received, the rescue got underway. Two Super Stallion helicopters, two Super Cobra helicopters, and four jet fighters took off from a ship in the Adriatic Sea. Each aircraft had a special job to do. The Super Stallions carried a total of 40 combat Marines. They would land and rescue O'Grady. The two Super Cobra gunships, armed with missiles and machine guns, would hover overhead and deal with any enemy who might show up. And the jets would provide additional air support.

9 As the choppers moved into position, the Marines aboard spotted a yellow smoke signal—O'Grady's sign. The Super Stallions landed within 50 yards of his hiding place. The 40 Marines piled out and formed a tight defensive circle. Moments later, O'Grady rushed out of the bushes. He appeared to be very cold, so one Marine gave him a blanket. Then he was helped into one of the choppers. From touchdown to takeoff, the rescue took less than two minutes. It was perfect—a "textbook" rescue.

10 Colonel Martin Berndt, the commander of the rescue team, later said, "To see him [Captain O'Grady] running through the brush covered with sweat, with his pistol in his hand making his way to the aircraft, [was] not a scene that I'll soon forget."

11 Still, the whole enterprise could have ended in disaster. After all, they were in Serb-held territory. Shortly after O'Grady was picked up, Serbs fired one or maybe two missiles at the choppers, but they both missed. The Serbs also fired on the choppers with automatic weapons. Luckily, they left nothing but a few holes; everyone escaped unharmed.

12 After O'Grady was safely back on American soil, President Bill Clinton called to congratulate him. The President also told the media that the pilot was "one amazing kid." But Captain Scott O'Grady saw things differently. To him, the real heroes were the men who came to rescue him. "They say they were just doing their job," he said. "But they risked their lives to get me out. If you want to find some heroes, that's where you should look."

If you have been timed while reading this article, enter your reading time below. Then turn to the Words-per-Minute Table on page 195 and look up your reading speed (words per minute). Enter your reading speed on the graph on page 196.

Reading Time: Lesson 17

2 : 49

Minutes   *Seconds*

A | Finding the Main Idea

One statement below expresses the main idea of the article. One statement is too general, or too broad. The other statement explains only part of the article; it is too narrow. Label the statements using the following key:

M—Main Idea   **B—Too Broad**   **N—Too Narrow**

__B__   1. One of the most frightening situations for any soldier is to be all alone behind enemy lines.

__N__   2. The exciting rescue of Scott O'Grady involved 40 aircraft, at least six ships, and more than 100 military personnel.

__M__   3. Scott O'Grady, a pilot trained in survival techniques, was rescued in Bosnia in a "picture perfect" mission

---

_____ Score 15 points for a correct M answer.

_____ Score 5 points for each correct B or N answer.

_____ **Total Score:** Finding the Main Idea

B | Recalling Facts

How well do you remember the facts in the article? Put an X in the box next to the answer that correctly completes each statement about the article.

1. SERE stands for
   - ☐ a. Staying Ever Ready to Escape.
   - ☐ b. Surviving Enemy Retaliation with Energy.
   - ☒ c. Survival, Evasion, Resistance, and Escape.

2. Captain O'Grady's jet fighter was shot down by
   - ☒ a. surface-to-air missiles.
   - ☐ b. machine gun fire from an enemy jet.
   - ☒ c. a missile shot from an enemy jet.

3. O'Grady landed in an area that was held by the
   - ☐ a. United States.
   - ☒ b. Serbs.
   - ☐ c. United Nations forces.

4. O'Grady did not use his radio for
   - ☒ a. over five days.
   - ☐ b. five hours.
   - ☐ c. at least two weeks.

5. The rescue team landed about
   - ☐ a. 5 miles from O'Grady's hiding place.
   - ☐ b. 100 yards from O'Grady's hiding place.
   - ☒ c. 50 yards from O'Grady's hiding place.

Score 5 points for each correct answer.

_____ **Total Score:** Recalling Facts

C Making Inferences

When you combine your own experience and information from a text to draw a conclusion that is not directly stated in that text, you are making an inference. Below are five statements that may or may not be inferences based on information in the article. Label the statements using the following key:

C—Correct Inference   **F—Faulty Inference**

_C_   1. Without the SERE training, O'Grady might well have died before he could be rescued.

_F_   2. Bosnia is a desert land with very few trees or bushes.

_F_   3. The rescue mission was poorly organized.

_C_   4. O'Grady kept a clear head while he was behind enemy lines.

_C_   5. O'Grady was hungry and tired when he was finally rescued.

Score 5 points for each correct answer.

_____ **Total Score:** Making Inferences

D Using Words Precisely

Each numbered sentence below contains an underlined word or phrase from the article. Following the sentence are three definitions. One definition is closest to the meaning of the underlined word. One definition is opposite or nearly opposite. Label those two definitions using the following key. Do not label the remaining definition.

C—Closest   **O—Opposite or Nearly Opposite**

1. And to <u>ward off</u> boredom, he played "entire rounds of golf and chess" in his mind.

   _C_   a. fight off

   ___   b. think about

   _O_   c. welcome

2. As the front section of the jet tumbled toward the ground, O'Grady pulled a special cord that blew away his canopy and <u>ejected</u> him from the cockpit.

   ___   a. photographed

   _O_   b. pulled in

   _C_   c. threw out

3. He fell face down on the ground and covered his head and ears with his <u>camouflaged</u> gloves to make himself harder to see.

   ___   a. given an artistic pattern

   _C_   b. patterned so as to be unnoticed

   _O_   c. patterned to be obvious

4. He had the necessary equipment to <u>evade</u> the enemy and to survive for several days....

_____ a. join

_____ b. battle

_____ c. stay away from

5. The two Super Cobra gunships, armed with missiles and machine guns, would <u>hover</u> overhead and deal with any enemy who might show up.

_____ a. land

_____ b. hang suspended in air

_____ c. make noise

_____ Score 3 points for each correct C answer.

_____ Score 2 points for each correct O answer.

_____ **Total Score:** Using Words Precisely

Enter the four total scores in the spaces below, and add them together to find your Reading Comprehension Score. Then record your score on the graph on page 197.

Score	Question Type	Lesson 17
_____	Finding the Main Idea	
_____	Recalling Facts	
_____	Making Inferences	
_____	Using Words Precisely	
_____	**Reading Comprehension Score**	

Author's Approach

Put an X in the box next to the correct answer.

1. The main purpose of the first paragraph is to
   ☐ a. describe the wilderness of Washington.
   ☒ b. explain how Scott O'Grady prepared for the adventure to follow.
   ☐ c. raise the reader's curiosity about the SERE course.

2. What is the author's purpose in writing "Shot Down Behind Enemy Lines"?
   ☐ a. To encourage the reader to take the SERE course
   ☒ b. To inform the reader about an exciting rescue
   ☐ c. To express an opinion about war

3. What does the author imply by saying "The Super Stallions landed within 50 yards of his [O'Grady's] hiding place"?
   ☒ a. It was fortunate that the helicopters landed so unbelievably close to O'Grady's hiding place.
   ☐ b. The helicopter pilots were careless and landed too far from O'Grady's hiding place to do any good.
   ☐ c. O'Grady was almost injured when the helicopters landed so close to his hiding place.

_____ Number of correct answers

Record your personal assessment of your work on the Critical Thinking Chart on page 198.

Summarizing and Paraphrasing

Put an X in the box next to the correct answer.

1. Below are summaries of the article. Choose the summary that says all the most important things about the article but in the fewest words.

☒ a. Captain Scott O'Grady, whose patrolling jet fighter was shot down over Serb-held Bosnia, used survival techniques to survive for several days. He finally radioed his call sign to indicate that he was still alive. A skilled team went to his aid and pulled off a "textbook" rescue.

☐ b. Serbs fired missiles at Captain Scott O'Grady and his fellow pilot, Captain Bob Wright during a routine air patrol. Wright was able to avoid the missiles but O'Grady was shot down. For several days, he survived, using only the items that he carried with him.

☐ c. An amazing rescue took place on June 8, 1995, when Scott O'Grady was rescued by a team of 40 aircraft, half a dozen ships, and more than 100 military personnel. O'Grady insisted that it was not he, but the rescuers, who were heroes.

2. Choose the best one-sentence paraphrase for the following sentence from the article:

"Captain Wright had last seen him [O'Grady] going down through the clouds and hadn't seen his parachute open."

☐ a. Without opening his parachute, Captain Wright saw O'Grady going down through the clouds.

☐ b. Captain Wright saw O'Grady last as he himself was parachuting down through the clouds.

☒ c. The last time Captain Wright had seen O'Grady, O'Grady had been falling through the sky without opening his parachute.

_____ Number of correct answers

Record your personal assessment of your work on the Critical Thinking Chart on page 198.

Critical Thinking

Put an X in the box next to the correct answer for questions 1, 3, and 4. Follow the directions provided for the other questions.

1. From what the article told about the value of SERE to Captain O'Grady, you can predict that the air force will

☐ a. discontinue the course.

☒ b. continue to offer the course to military personnel.

☐ c. offer the course free to any U.S. citizen, military or nonmilitary, who would like to take it.

2. Choose from the letters below to correctly complete the following statement. Write the letters on the lines.

In the article, ____C____ and ____B____ are alike.

a. the goal of Colonel Martin Berndt's mission

b. the goal of Captain Wright's mission

c. the goal of Captain O'Grady's mission

3. What was the effect of Captain O'Grady's radio silence for over five days?

☒ a. No one knew whether he was alive or dead.

☐ b. O'Grady was able to sleep more soundly than he would have with the radio operating.

☐ c. The radio had been damaged.

4. Of the following theme categories, which one (or ones) would this story fit into?

☒ a. Always be prepared.

☒ b. Keep your head in times of crisis.

☐ c. Always follow the path of least resistance.

5. In which paragraph did you find your information or details to answer question 3?

_____

_____

_____ Number of correct answers   Record your personal assessment of your work on the Critical Thinking Chart on page 198.

Personal Response

I agree with the author because

_____

_____

_____

_____

A word or phrase in the article that I do not understand is

_____

_____

_____

_____

_____

ADRIFT WITH NO HOPE

The Rescuers: Paul Murray, Vance Bunker, and Rick Kohls gave up the warmth and security of their homes to save three men from the frigid and dangerous Atlantic Ocean off the Maine coast in January 1992.

The North Atlantic Ocean shimmered in the early morning sun off the coast of Maine. It was January 16, 1992, and the winter air was bitingly cold. But with a clear blue sky and a calm sea, it looked like it would be a routine voyage for Rudi Musetti, the captain of the *Harkness*. Musetti's job was to sail the tugboat from Eliot, on the southern tip of Maine, up the coast to Northeast Harbor. The planned 22-hour sail, however, would turn out to be anything but routine.

2   On this morning, Arthur Stevens joined Musetti on the tugboat. Stevens, an experienced sailor, invited Duane Cleaves, an old buddy, to go along just for the ride. "We've got nothing in common," Cleaves joked about Stevens, "He's ocean, and I'm a 'tater guy [potato grower] from Aroostock [County]."

3   The trip began smoothly enough, but around midday the sea grew ugly. Musetti and Stevens wondered how well Cleaves would hold up. The rolling and pitching of the tugboat didn't seem to bother the potato farmer, however; Cleaves kept

himself busy cleaning the galley. Then, late in the afternoon with the tugboat well out to sea, the ocean turned really nasty. Fierce winds plunged the wind chill down to 54 degrees below zero. Every inch of the tugboat's exterior was covered with ice. A six-foot layer of smothering fog called "sea smoke" floated on the surface of the water. This fog was so thick that it was hard for the men to see their hands in front of their faces.

4 Then, to his horror, Musetti noticed more than a foot of water sloshing over the deck. Somehow the *Harkness* had sprung a leak and was taking on water fast. Musetti hurried into the engine room and tried to turn on the bilge pump, but it was frozen solid. At that moment, a huge swell hit the tugboat broadside, washing 600 feet of thick tow rope over the side. Now Musetti had an additional problem: he had to steer the Harkness straight or else run the risk that the dangling rope would snarl the propellers and kill the tug's two engines.

5 At 6:05 P.M. Musetti radioed the Coast Guard. "I've got a foot and a half of water on the stern…" he said. "I'm going to try for Frenchboro." (Frenchboro was a port 20 miles to the north of his present location.)

6 Meanwhile, Dave Allen, an old boyhood chum of Musetti's, was listening to his radio scanner on Vinalhaven Island. "Don't try for Frenchboro," he radioed Musetti. "Head to Matinicus. If anyone can find you, it's the fishermen of Matinicus."

7 Musetti was only five miles away from Matinicus, but he had thought that the two-mile-long island was deserted in the winter. In fact, 10 families made this island on the rim of Penobscot Bay their year-round home. With his ice-coated radar now worthless, Musetti felt he had no choice; he turned for Matinicus. But, just as he had feared, the tow ropes swept under the tugboat and wrapped around the propellers, killing the engines. Now without power, the tug bobbed up and down, helpless in the raging sea. By 7 P.M. the water in the pilothouse had reached Musetti's chest. He radioed the Coast Guard with the message, "We're going down."

8 Meanwhile, all along the Maine coast, people had been listening on their scanners to the unfolding drama at sea. On Matinicus, Rick and Sue Kohls were having supper at Vance and Sari Bunker's house. Like many fishermen, they had their scanner turned on in the background. They heard Musetti radio the Coast Guard; they knew that the Coast Guard had sent a ship to the rescue. But they also knew that it would take the ship a long time to reach the *Harkness*.

9 Rick Kohls and Vance Bunker just nodded to each other. Then they left the dinner table and put on their foul weather gear with no questions asked. Along the coast of Maine it is an unwritten law that when somebody calls for help, you don't ask whether you should go—you only ask how to get there. At 6:40 P.M., Paul Murray, a neighbor, joined Kohls and

The Rescued: Rudi Musetti, Arthur Stevens, and Duane Cleaves were saved from drowning in the icy waters of the Atlantic.

Bunker on Bunker's boat, the *Jan-Ellen*. Bunker radioed Musetti to inform him that help was on the way. But when he heard Musetti's last radio message saying the tugboat was going down, all of the would-be rescuers felt certain that if they found anything at all, it would be dead men. They knew that no one survives for more than a few minutes in the frigid Atlantic in January. But they had to give it a try anyway.

10   Back on the *Harkness*, Musetti, Stevens, and Cleaves were wiggling into their thinly-insulated immersion suits. The suits were designed to protect seamen from the shock of cold water if they slipped overboard in the winter. The suits would not keep the crew of the *Harkness* warm for long, but they were better than nothing. The men got the suits on just in time, for minutes later a large wave washed Musetti, Stevens, and Cleaves over the side. Luckily, an eight-foot wooden ladder from the tug was also washed overboard. Somehow, despite the sea smoke and the dark night, the three men found each other and the ladder. "Stay together, boys," cried Musetti, "we've got to stay together." In his heart, however, he knew that they would all be dead soon.

After all, what chance did they really have of being spotted with all that sea smoke and darkness?

11   Still on their way, the men on the Coast Guard boat and the *Jan-Ellen* studied the situation. They guessed that the tug must have gone down somewhere near the ledges of No Man's Land and Zephyr Rock, a mile and a half northeast of Matinicus. Both boats arrived at that spot at about the same time. But where were Musetti, Stevens, and Cleaves?

12   The rescuers' searchlights were useless. The powerful light beams bounced back off the sea smoke vapors, blinding the searchers. The boats moved very slowly through the water as the men on board scanned the surface below. In the water, Stevens saw the running lights of the *Jan-Ellen*, but was too weak to shout. Then, incredibly, the two boats edged straight for him. When Musetti saw the lights, he thought for a moment he was hallucinating. "Maybe they were angels," he remembered thinking, "coming to get me and the others." But when the "angels" began to shout and reach down to grab him, he realized it wasn't a dream.

13   The crew of the *Jan-Ellen* hauled Musetti and Cleaves into the boat, while

the Coast Guard rescued Stevens. How did the rescuers find them in zero visibility? It seems that when the *Harkness* began to sink, Cleaves grabbed a flashlight which then froze to his glove. When he hit the water, he was too numb to hold the flashlight but it stuck to his glove anyway. The beam from that flashlight penetrated the sea smoke just enough for Kohls to see it.

14   It later turned out that the flashlight didn't belong to Cleaves. It was Stevens's. His 16-year-old daughter, Robyn, had given it to him as a Christmas gift. That was some gift—it not only saved his life but the lives of his two buddies as well. 🍃

If you have been timed while reading this article, enter your reading time below. Then turn to the Words-per-Minute Table on page 195 and look up your reading speed (words per minute). Enter your reading speed on the graph on page 196.

Reading Time: Lesson 18

___1___ : ___85___

Minutes   Seconds

A Finding the Main Idea

One statement below expresses the main idea of the article. One statement is too general, or too broad. The other statement explains only part of the article; it is too narrow. Label the statements using the following key:

M—Main Idea   **B—Too Broad**   **N—Too Narrow**

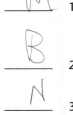

_M_ 1. A series of disasters seemed to mean certain death for three men trapped on a sinking tugboat in the Atlantic, however, the men were rescued just in time.

_B_ 2. Sailing the Atlantic can be dangerous at any time of the year, but especially in January.

_N_ 3. Already battling a wind chill of about 54 degrees below zero, the captain of the *Harkness* was horrified to spot another problem—his boat was taking on water.

_____ Score 15 points for a correct M answer.

_____ Score 5 points for each correct B or N answer.

_____ **Total Score:** Finding the Main Idea

B Recalling Facts

How well do you remember the facts in the article? Put an X in the box next to the answer that correctly completes each statement about the article.

1. The tugboat *Harkness* was headed to
   ☒ a. Eliot, Maine.
   ☒ b. Northeast Harbor, Maine.
   ☐ c. Boston, Massachusetts.

2. Sea smoke is
   ☒ a. thick fog floating on the water's surface.
   ☐ b. exhaust from the tugboat's engines.
   ☐ c. pollution put out by factories on the coast.

3. When Musetti turned the boat to head for Matinicus,
   ☐ a. his radio stopped working.
   ☐ b. Stevens and Cleaves were washed overboard.
   ☒ c. the tow ropes tangled in the propellers.

4. Rick Kohls, Vance Bunker, and Paul Murray lived
   ☐ a. on Matinicus.
   ☒ b. in Northeast Harbor.
   ☐ c. in Frenchboro.

5. The rescuers located the men when they saw
   ☐ a. the ladder the men were clinging to.
   ☒ b. a flashlight's beam.
   ☐ c. Musetti waving to them.

Score 5 points for each correct answer.

_____ **Total Score:** Recalling Facts

C | Making Inferences

When you combine your own experience and information from a text to draw a conclusion that is not directly stated in that text, you are making an inference. Below are five statements that may or may not be inferences based on information in the article. Label the statements using the following key:

C—Correct Inference   **F—Faulty Inference**

_____ 1. All the men onboard the *Harkness* were glad that Stevens had brought along his flashlight.

_____ 2. The leak on the *Harkness* would probably not have been quite as dangerous if the weather had been warm.

_____ 3. If it is sunny and calm in the early morning, you can be sure that the weather will stay pleasant all day.

_____ 4. Generally, the Coast Guard can be counted on to help in emergencies at sea.

_____ 5. Radio scanners on Matinicus don't work properly whenever there is stormy weather.

Score 5 points for each correct answer.

_____ **Total Score:** Making Inferences

D | Using Words Precisely

Each numbered sentence below contains an underlined word or phrase from the article. Following the sentence are three definitions. One definition is closest to the meaning of the underlined word. One definition is opposite or nearly opposite. Label those two definitions using the following key. Do not label the remaining definition.

C—Closest   **O—Opposite or Nearly Opposite**

1. The North Atlantic Ocean <u>shimmered</u> in the early morning sun off the coast of Maine.

_____ a. shone in wavering, fitful way

 b. shone steadily

_____ c. shone dimly

2. At that moment, a huge swell hit the tugboat <u>broadside</u>, washing 600 feet of thick tow rope over the side.

_____ a. violently

_____ b. along its side

 c. from the front

3. They knew that no one survives for more than a few minutes in the <u>frigid</u> Atlantic in January.

_____ a. treacherous

_____ b. warm

_____ c. extremely cold

4. Back on the *Harkness*, Musetti, Stevens, and Cleaves were wiggling into their thinly-insulated <u>immersion</u> suits.

_____ a. coming out of or emerging

_____ b. heating something

_____ c. plunging or submerging

5. When Musetti saw the lights, he thought for a moment he was <u>hallucinating</u>.

_____ a. seeing reality clearly

_____ b. having visions

_____ c. falling

_____ Score 3 points for each correct C answer.

_____ Score 2 points for each correct O answer.

_____ **Total Score:** Using Words Precisely

Enter the four total scores in the spaces below, and add them together to find your Reading Comprehension Score. Then record your score on the graph on page 197.

Score	Question Type	Lesson 18
_____	Finding the Main Idea	
_____	Recalling Facts	
_____	Making Inferences	
_____	Using Words Precisely	
_____	**Reading Comprehension Score**	

Author's Approach

Put an X in the box next to the correct answer.

1. The author uses the first sentence of the article to

☐ a. inform the reader about an exciting rescue.

☐ b. describe the qualities of one January morning in Maine.

☐ c. surprise the reader with an unusual comparison.

2. In this article, "The trip began smoothly enough, but around midday the sea grew ugly" means

☐ a. although the men were having a good time at the beginning of the trip, they soon began to feel upset and angry with each other.

☐ b. the sea was calm when the trip started, but it started getting rough and dangerous around midday.

☐ c. the men enjoyed the beauty of the sea when they began the trip, but they thought that it began to look unattractive around midday.

3. Choose the statement below that best describes the author's position in paragraph 9.

☐ a. Kohls, Bunker, and Murray resented having to go out on such a bad night knowing that the people they had hoped to rescue were already dead.

☐ b. People in Maine are better neighbors than people in any other region of the country.

☐ c. The men who set out to rescue the *Harkness* were genuinely concerned about the welfare of those in trouble.

_____ Number of correct answers

Record your personal assessment of your work on the Critical Thinking Chart on page 198.

Summarizing and Paraphrasing

Follow the directions provided for questions 1 and 2. Put an X in the box next to the correct answer for the other question.

1. Look for the important ideas and events in paragraphs 5 and 6. Summarize those paragraphs in one or two sentences.

   _____

   _____

   _____

2. Complete the following one-sentence summary of the article using the lettered phrases from the phrase bank below. Write the letters on the lines.

   > **Phrase Bank:**
   >
   > a. the rescue of the men aboard the Harkness and the reason why they were spotted
   >
   > b. the beginning of the *Harkness*'s trip
   >
   > c. all the problems the tugboat ran into

   The article "Adrift with No Hope" begins with _____, goes on to explain _____, and ends with _____.

3. Choose the sentence that correctly restates the following sentence from the article:

   "But, just as he [Musetti] had feared, the tow ropes swept under the tugboat and wrapped around the propellers, killing the engines."

   ☒ a. Musetti was afraid that the tow ropes might sweep under the tugboat and destroy the propellers.

   ☐ b. The tow ropes moved under the boat, tangled themselves in the propellers, and stopped the engines from working, just as Musetti had dreaded they might.

   ☐ c. Musetti hoped that the two ropes would go under the boat and wrap around the propellers.

   _____ Number of correct answers

   Record your personal assessment of your work on the Critical Thinking Chart on page 198.

Critical Thinking

Follow the directions provided for questions 1 and 3. Put an X in the box next to the correct answer for the other questions.

1. For each statement below, write O if it expresses an opinion or write F if it expresses a fact.

   _____ a. Musetti tried to work the bilge pump, but it was frozen solid.

   _____ b. Musetti was foolish to have taken his tugboat out in the middle of January.

   _____ c. Ten families lived on Matinicus Island year-round.

2. Judging by the events in the article, you can predict that the following will happen next:

☐ a.   Cleaves will decide to give up farming and take up sailing.

☐ b.   the Coast Guard will scold the men from Matinicus for going out on a night with such bad weather.

☒ c.   the rescued men will be taken to a hospital.

3. Choose from the letters below to correctly complete the following statement. Write the letters on the lines.

In the article, ___A___ and ___B___ are different.

a.   the environment in which Cleaves worked

b.   the environment in which Stevens worked

c.   the environment in which Musetti worked

4. What was the cause of the tow rope's ending up in the water?

☐ a.   It was placed in the water at the beginning of the trip.

☐ b.   A giant wave washed it overboard.

☐ c.   Musetti threw it overboard during the trip.

_____ Number of correct answers

Record your personal assessment of your work on the Critical Thinking Chart on page 198.

Personal Response

I wonder why

_____

_____

_____

_____

Self-Assessment

From reading this article, I have learned

_____

_____

_____

_____

CRITICAL THINKING

RESCUE DOWN UNDER

"he first thing I heard was a massive roaring sound, like a massive wind coming down the valley," recalled 27-year-old Stuart Diver, a ski instructor. "I woke up and thought it was a hailstorm.... And then [there were sounds] like bombs going off one after the other as all the concrete and metal and everything twisted down and fell on top of us."

2   At 9:00 P.M. on July 30, 1997, Stuart Diver and his wife Sally had gone to bed. The Divers lived in the Bimbadeen Lodge in the ski resort town of Thredbo, Australia. It was about 11:30 that night when the "massive roaring" began. But the noise wasn't caused by a hailstorm or a bombing. The sound Diver heard was the mountain above his lodge giving way. In just a few seconds, the monstrous landslide swept away everything in its path—trees, rocks, cars, and two ski lodges. Nineteen people, including Diver and his wife, were buried in the violent onslaught of mud, water, and debris.

3   Within 10 minutes, rescue workers had rushed to the scene and set up emergency lights. Beneath the enormous pile of rubble, rescue workers could hear faint cries for help. But the cries soon faded

Rescue workers look through the ruins of the ski lodges destroyed in the landslide at Thredbo, Australia.

out, and for the next two days searchers didn't hear a single sound of life. Neighbors and relatives of those trapped by the sudden landslide complained that rescue workers were not moving fast enough. But the workers did the best they could. Time after time, their instruments indicated that the earth might shift again. One man at the scene said, "When you

see the site, it's bloody obvious [why the rescue workers didn't go faster.] Hurrying would just get you killed." Also, the scale of the damage convinced officials that the chances of finding anyone alive were "infinitesimally small."

4   Yet, beneath the rubble, not everyone was dead. Stuart and Sally Diver had survived the initial landslide. They had

Rescue workers attempt to reach trapped ski instructor Stuart Diver.

become trapped between slabs of concrete, but fortunately two metal reinforcing bars kept the concrete from falling and crushing them. Still, they were caught in a space so small it was almost impossible to move. This was particularly true for Sally, who was pinned to the bed and badly hurt.

5   Their concrete tomb couldn't stop water from trickling in, and since this was the middle of winter in Australia, the water was frigid. To make matters worse, Stuart was wearing nothing but his boxer shorts. As the water streamed over the Divers, Stuart felt around in the darkness and took hold of Sally's head, lifting it up so she could breath. Soon, however, the rubble shifted and Sally slipped out of his grasp. Before he could say goodbye, the water covered his helpless wife's face and she was dead.

6   Remarkably, this tragedy seemed to strengthen Stuart's resolve to stay alive. He later said he was thinking, "I've got to hold myself up out of this water and...try to put my head in this little air pocket so that I can live." But would Stuart be found before he, too, drowned or was swept away by further earth movement? Would he be found before he died from hypothermia under 25 feet of rubble?

7   Back up on the surface, officials had launched the largest rescue operation in the history of Australia. They brought in sniffing dogs, sensitive listening devices, and infrared cameras to detect body heat below. They formed a human chain to clear the debris away piece by piece. All this was done with the sad belief that no one was still alive and with the constant fear of another major landslide.

8   After nearly 55 hours, just as rescuers were close to giving up all hope, one of them thought he heard a faint sound. All other work immediately ceased, and all the generators were shut off. Everyone just stood frozen in silence. It was so perfectly quiet you could hear a pin drop. Then the rescue worker shouted, "Rescue team working overhead, can anyone hear me?"

9   "I can hear you," the rescuers heard Stuart answer.

10   Charlie Sanderson, the police superintendent of Thredbo, told the media, "A miracle has occurred."

11   If finding Stuart Diver was a miracle, it would take a second miracle to get him out. One false step and the concrete slabs could fall and crush him. On the other hand, the rescuers had to work fast or the water might fill the pocket of air that was keeping Stuart alive. In addition, there was the possibility that he would simply freeze to death before they reached him. His body temperature had already dipped to a life-threatening 88 degrees.

12   Knowing it was vital to keep up Stuart's spirits, paramedic Paul Featherstone called out a stream of hopeful chatter. Even when the rubble became unstable and the area had to be briefly abandoned, Featherstone stayed with Stuart, pretending nothing was wrong. "Don't worry, mate, we're all back here. We're cutting you out," he shouted, banging a shovel on a rock so Stuart would think the rescue workers were still there.

13   Finally, after more than 10 daunting hours of drilling, rescue workers opened a hole big enough to pull Stuart through. He had been trapped in his pitch-black tomb with his nose pressed against a concrete slab for 65 hours. As he blinked his eyes in the brightness of the daylight, he glanced upward. "That sky is fantastic," he said. Amazingly, Stuart suffered only some cuts and bruises, frostbite, and a mild case of hypothermia.

14   Finding Stuart encouraged the rescue workers to keep looking for even more survivors. As firefighter Ian Krimmer said, "Every rescue worker's philosophy is that you never give up hope until you remove that last piece of debris." Sadly, there would be no more miracles at Thredbo. Stuart Diver was the only person to survive this disaster.

If you have been timed while reading this article, enter your reading time below. Then turn to the Words-per-Minute Table on page 195 and look up your reading speed (words per minute). Enter your reading speed on the graph on page 196.

Reading Time: Lesson 19

_____ : _____
Minutes   Seconds

A | Finding the Main Idea

One statement below expresses the main idea of the article. One statement is too general, or too broad. The other statement explains only part of the article; it is too narrow. Label the statements using the following key:

M—Main Idea   **B—Too Broad**   **N—Too Narrow**

_____ 1. A huge landslide in Australia covered Stuart and Sally Diver with debris; Sally died, but Stuart was finally rescued after being trapped under rubble for 65 hours.

_____ 2. Rescuers in Thredbo, Australia, worked furiously to save landslide victims even though their instruments indicated that the earth might shift again at any time.

_____ 3. Landslides sometimes happen so quickly that their victims are not able to escape in time.

_____ Score 15 points for a correct M answer.

_____ Score 5 points for each correct B or N answer.

_____ **Total Score:** Finding the Main Idea

B | Recalling Facts

How well do you remember the facts in the article? Put an X in the box next to the answer that correctly completes each statement about the article.

1. Thredbo, Australia, is a
   - ☐ a. major industrial city.
   - ☒ b. beach community.
   - ☐ c. ski resort.

2. Rescue workers arrived on the scene of the disaster
   - ☒ a. 24 hours after the landslide happened.
   - ☐ b. within 10 minutes of the landslide.
   - ☐ c. almost 10 hours after the landslide.

3. The landslide occurred during the
   - ☐ a. middle of winter.
   - ☒ b. middle of summer.
   - ☐ c. spring.

4. Sally died
   - ☒ a. during the landslide.
   - ☐ b. after she bled to death.
   - ☐ c. when the rubble shifted and Stuart couldn't hold her head up out of the water anymore.

5. Stuart was finally rescued after
   - ☒ a. workers removed all the debris on top of him.
   - ☐ b. workers drilled a hole big enough to pull him through.
   - ☐ c. he worked his way free of the debris and crawled to the surface.

Score 5 points for each correct answer.

_____ **Total Score:** Recalling Facts

C Making Inferences

When you combine your own experience and information from a text to draw a conclusion that is not directly stated in that text, you are making an inference. Below are five statements that may or may not be inferences based on information in the article. Label the statements using the following key:

C—Correct Inference   F—Faulty Inference

_____ 1. If rescue workers had arrived at the scene more quickly, many more victims could have been saved.

_____ 2. Sally and Stuart Diver were the only victims who became trapped beneath landslide debris.

_____ 3. To stay healthy, humans need to maintain a temperature higher than 88 degrees.

_____ 4. When Stuart emerged from his "tomb," he appreciated normal, natural sights more than he had before his ordeal.

_____ 5. Just before the disaster, geologists had predicted the Thredbo landslide and had told residents to evacuate, but the Divers had ignored their advice.

Score 5 points for each correct answer.

_____ **Total Score:** Making Inferences

D Using Words Precisely

Each numbered sentence below contains an underlined word or phrase from the article. Following the sentence are three definitions. One definition is closest to the meaning of the underlined word. One definition is opposite or nearly opposite. Label those two definitions using the following key. Do not label the remaining definition.

C—Closest   O—Opposite or Nearly Opposite

1. In just a few seconds, the <u>monstrous</u> landslide swept away everything in its path—trees, rocks, cars, and two ski lodges.

_____ a. miniature

_____ b. roaring

_____ c. gigantic

2. Would he be found before he died from <u>hypothermia</u> under 25 feet of rubble?

_____ a. below-normal body temperature

_____ b. starvation

_____ c. above-normal body temperature

3. They brought in sniffing dogs, sensitive listening devices, and infrared cameras to <u>detect</u> body heat below.

_____ a. lose track of

_____ b. find

_____ c. cool down

4. Knowing it was <u>vital</u> to keep up Stuart's spirits, paramedic Paul Featherstone called out a stream of hopeful chatter.

_____ a. absolutely essential

_____ b. convenient

_____ c. not important

5. Finally, after more than 10 <u>daunting</u> hours of drilling, rescue workers opened a hole big enough to pull Stuart through.

_____ a. long

_____ b. hope-filled

_____ c. discouraging

_____ Score 3 points for each correct C answer.

_____ Score 2 points for each correct O answer.

_____ **Total Score:** Using Words Precisely

Enter the four total scores in the spaces below, and add them together to find your Reading Comprehension Score. Then record your score on the graph on page 197.

Score	Question Type	Lesson 19
_____	Finding the Main Idea	
_____	Recalling Facts	
_____	Making Inferences	
_____	Using Words Precisely	
_____	**Reading Comprehension Score**	

Author's Approach

Put an X in the box next to the correct answer.

1. The main purpose of the first paragraph is to
   - ☐ a. describe what it was like to live through a landslide.
   - ☐ b. explain how Stuart Diver got caught in the landslide.
   - ☐ c. explain how the landslide got started.

2. Judging by statements from the article "Rescue Down Under," you can conclude that the author wants the reader to think that
   - ☐ a. rescuers did all they could under the circumstances.
   - ☐ b. rescuers could have tried harder to rescue more people.
   - ☐ c. Paul Featherstone was the only rescuer who really cared about his work.

3. What does the author imply by saying "Charlie Sanderson, the police superintendent of Thredbo, told the media, 'A miracle has occurred'" after the rescuers heard a voice from beneath the rubble?
   - ☐ a. Charlie Sanderson thought that a dead person was speaking.
   - ☐ b. Charlie Sanderson was a religious man.
   - ☐ c. No one had expected to find anyone alive under the rubble.

_____ Number of correct answers

Record your personal assessment of your work on the Critical Thinking Chart on page 198.

Summarizing and Paraphrasing

Follow the directions provided for questions 1 and 2. Put an X in the box next to the correct answer for question 3.

1. Complete the following one-sentence summary of the article using the lettered phrases from the phrase bank below. Write the letters on the lines.

> **Phrase Bank:**
>
> a. the rescue workers' continuing efforts to save more survivors and the failure to find any
>
> b. the death of Sally Diver and the rescue of Stuart Diver
>
> c. a description of the experience of being caught in a landslide

The article about "Rescue Down Under" begins with_____, goes on to explain_____, and ends with_____.

2. Reread paragraph 8 in the article. Below, write a summary of the paragraph in no more than 25 words.

_____

_____

_____

Reread your summary and decide whether it covers the important ideas in the paragraph. Next, decide how to shorten the summary to 15 words or less without leaving out any essential information. Write this summary below.

_____

_____

3. Read the statement about the article below. Then read the paraphrase of that statement. Choose the reason that best tells why the paraphrase does not say the same thing as the statement.

Statement: It took 10 hours for rescue workers to drill a hole large enough to pull Stuart Diver through.

Paraphrase: Stuart Diver was happy that rescue workers hadn't given up on him, although they took 10 hours to drill the hole they finally pulled him through.

☐ a. Paraphrase says too much.

☐ b. Paraphrase doesn't say enough.

☐ c. Paraphrase doesn't agree with the statement about the article.

_____ Number of correct answers

Record your personal assessment of your work on the Critical Thinking Chart on page 198.

Critical Thinking

Follow the directions provided for questions 1 and 5. Put an X in the box next to the correct answer for the other questions.

1. Choose from the letters below to correctly complete the following statement. Write the letters on the lines.

On the positive side, _____, but on the negative side _____.

a. workers were able to rescue Stuart Diver

b. Sally Diver died before rescuers could reach her

c. The landslide sounded like a massive wind

2. What was the effect of Paul Featherstone's banging a shovel on a rock?

☐ a. The noise made Stuart believe that rescuers were constantly working to free him.

☐ b. The noise scared away rodents.

☐ c. The noise kept Stuart awake and conscious.

3. How is "Rescue Down Under" related to the theme of this book?

☐ a. The article describes heroes who deserve credit for their deeds.

☐ b. The article describes a terrible natural disaster.

☐ c. The article describes a situation in which rescuers worked hard to save the life of one man.

4. If you were a rescue worker after a landslide, how could you use the information in the article to locate survivors?

☐ a. Unlike the Australian rescue workers, understand that you might as well give up the search after two days because it's unlikely that anyone could survive any longer than that.

☐ b. Like the Australian rescue workers did, use sniffing dogs, listening devices, and infrared cameras, and have everyone listen carefully.

☐ c. Don't bother with fancy gadgets; just ask one person to listen carefully while other workers move the debris.

5. In which paragraph did you find your information or details to answer question 2?

_____

_____ Number of correct answers

Record your personal assessment of your work on the Critical Thinking Chart on page 198.

Personal Response

I know the feeling that Stuart Diver had when he was trapped under the landslide debris because

_____

_____

_____

_____

Self-Assessment

What concepts or ideas from the article were difficult to understand?

_____

_____

_____

_____

Which were easy to understand?

_____

_____

_____

_____

CRITICAL THINKING

NEAR DEATH IN A RAIL YARD

The train's out of control," radioed the engineer of the Burlington Northern train. "You'd better get me lined up all the way through."

2   The freight train, with 89 cars, had left the Northtown rail yard in Minneapolis at 11:15 P.M. on February 14, 1996. It was headed for Galesburg, Illinois. A short time later, the engineer discovered that his brakes were gone. The 17-million pound train was gaining speed as it headed downhill into St. Paul.

3   Scary, yes, but this runaway train should not have posed a threat to anyone. There was no danger as long as the Burlington Northern was indeed "lined up all the way through." That meant keeping it on the main track, where it would zoom harmlessly past the rail yard in St. Paul at about 50 miles per hour. Finally, the train would coast to a stop on the next uphill grade and all would be well.

4   Rick Michalski, sitting in the St. Paul rail yard tower, heard over his two-way radio that a runaway train was headed his way. He wasn't overly concerned. The train was going to pass *outside* his rail yard. Michalski's job was to monitor train traffic *inside* the yard.

5   But suddenly Michalski saw a bright headlight coming into the yard from the west. He hadn't given anyone permission to use that section of track. Then Michalski heard a voice over his radio shouting, "You've got a train coming into the yard like a bat out of hell!"

6   The runaway Burlington Northern was barreling into the yard at high speed. One of the switches on the tracks had been improperly set, so the train was not "lined up all the way through." Instead, at 11:51 P.M., it came speeding into the St. Paul rail yard. At that time, workers inside the yard were going about their normal business. Engineer Gary LaValley was in his locomotive. Like Michalski, he had no time to react. The runaway crashed into the yard, sending other trains and debris flying everywhere. The violent chain reaction of jackknifing railroad cars lasted about 20 seconds. "So this is what it is to die," LaValley said to himself as debris rained down on his cab. Incredibly, though, he escaped with little more than a dislocated shoulder and some bruises.

7   His conductor wasn't so lucky. Rich Vitek had just stepped out of the yard office when he glanced up and down the tracks. Seeing that one bright headlight heading into the yard, he felt a blast of fear. All Vitek could do was turn and fall to the ground. "I just hoped I was in the right place," he later said.

8   The train collided with another engine that happened to be sitting on the tracks. Pushing that engine ahead of it, the Burlington Northern passed over Vitek's head. The two engines crashed through one end of the wooden yard office building. Vitek wasn't killed, but he was buried under a 20-foot-high pile of 2 × 8 beams,

Rich Vitek survived the accident despite being trapped for three hours under a pile of debris, including a railroad car loaded with soybeans.

A worker drains fuel from the engine of the Burlington Northern train that lost its brakes and slammed into a railroad office building in St. Paul, Minnesota.

railroad ties, and debris. A railroad car loaded with soybeans ended up at the top of the pile, and a hole in that car sent soybeans streaming steadily down over the wreckage.

9   All anyone could see of Vitek were his feet. He lay face down at the bottom of the pile, his right arm trapped beneath his chest. The mountain of debris pinned him so flat that he could lift his head only three inches. Dripping diesel fuel began to seep underneath his head, and the soybeans piled up around him, threatening to suffocate him. "We called to him," said captain Don Eddy, one of the St. Paul firefighters who quickly arrived on the scene. "He moved his feet to show that he was alive."

10   Although he wasn't dead, Vitek was in pretty bad shape. He had to hold his breath whenever he dropped his face into the rancid pool of diesel fuel. And he needed to lower his head often to relieve the agony in his injured neck. "He [kept] telling me that he was going to die," remembered Eddy. "But I told him everything was secure and that it would take some time, but we were going to get him out of there."

11   First, the rescuers jammed lumber into the hole in the grain car to stop the leaking soybeans. Then they used two small hydraulic jacks to prevent the pile of debris from crushing Vitek. They even managed to lift the pile a little bit—but not nearly enough to extricate Vitek, who

had fallen into a slight depression in the ground.

12   The problem was how to dig out Vitek without causing the pile to collapse and kill him. Electrical equipment couldn't be used because it might spark a fire. Picks, crowbars, and shovels were impossible to maneuver in the tiny opening next to Vitek. At last, someone suggested using an air-powered chisel to dig a hole in the ground next to Vitek. When the hole was big enough, the rescuers hoped, they would be able to slide Vitek out.

13   It was a long shot and would take hours to do. The chisel would have to chip away ground that was frozen solid from the harsh Minnesota winter. When Eddy crawled on his belly to communicate the plan to Vitek and to encourage him to hold on a little longer, Vitek replied, "Why don't you guys just give it up? You're not getting me out of here."

14   Despite his words of gloom, Rich Vitek somehow summoned the courage to hang on. "Every time I lost faith, I saw the faces of my family," he later recalled. "They reminded me of how much I had to live for."

15   Eddy and three other rescuers took 20-minute turns working the one-inch blade on the air drill. Every few minutes, they had to scoop away loose dirt with one hand. It was tedious work and progress was slow, but after three hours of painstaking drilling the rescuers had chiseled an opening wide enough for Vitek's body.

Using all his strength, Vitek managed to squeeze part of his body into the hole. "Pull me out!" he shouted.

16   "Then several of us grabbed his coveralls and slid him, slowly, feet first, out from under," said Eddy. Vitek, his eyes swollen shut from the diesel fuel, was rushed to the hospital.

17   Although he suffered nerve damage and spinal disk problems, Rich Vitek was alive, thanks to the efforts of Eddy and the others. Don Eddy was later asked about the dangers of such a rescue. "I worried that the 2×8s [the beams] might snap and trap someone else under there," he answered. "And we were cold, very cold. The fuel oil soaked through our gear and our clothes underneath. But we were focused on what we had to do." 🍃

If you have been timed while reading this article, enter your reading time below. Then turn to the Words-per-Minute Table on page 195 and look up your reading speed (words per minute). Enter your reading speed on the graph on page 196.

Reading Time: Lesson 20

_____ : _____
Minutes   Seconds

A | Finding the Main Idea

One statement below expresses the main idea of the article. One statement is too general, or too broad. The other statement explains only part of the article; it is too narrow. Label the statements using the following key:

M—Main Idea   **B—Too Broad**   **N—Too Narrow**

_____ 1. Rich Vitek was buried under a 20-foot-high pile of beams, railroad ties, debris, and soybeans.

_____ 2. After a runaway train buried Rich Vitek under a 20-foot-high pile of debris, his own determination and that of the rescue workers helped him survive.

_____ 3. Sometimes danger can descend upon you suddenly, as Rich Vitek discovered.

_____ Score 15 points for a correct M answer.

_____ Score 5 points for each correct B or N answer.

_____ **Total Score:** Finding the Main Idea

B | Recalling Facts

How well do you remember the facts in the article? Put an X in the box next to the answer that correctly completes each statement about the article.

1. The engineer of the Burlington Northern discovered that his train had no brakes just before he entered
   ☐ a.   Minneapolis, Minnesota.
   ☐ b.   St. Paul, Minnesota.
   ☐ c.   Galesburg, Illinois.

2. The runaway train ended up in the busy rail yard because
   ☐ a.   a switch had been set improperly.
   ☐ b.   the engineer made a mistake.
   ☐ c.   that was its regularly scheduled stop.

3. When Rich Vitek saw the train, he
   ☐ a.   turned and fell to the ground.
   ☐ b.   ran away as fast as he could.
   ☐ c.   froze in fear.

4. Vitek was pinned under the debris
   ☐ a.   on his back.
   ☐ b.   in a sitting position.
   ☐ c.   on his stomach.

5. Rescuers saved Vitek by
   ☐ a.   chiseling a hole next to Vitek for him to slide into.
   ☐ b.   removing all the debris from on top of him.
   ☐ c.   digging a tunnel underneath him.

Score 5 points for each correct answer.

_____ **Total Score:** Recalling Facts

C   Making Inferences

When you combine your own experience and information from a text to draw a conclusion that is not directly stated in that text, you are making an inference. Below are five statements that may or may not be inferences based on information in the article. Label the statements using the following key:

C—Correct Inference   **F—Faulty Inference**

_____   1. Vitek loved his family.

_____   2. No one who worked for the rail yard had any previous experience with runaway trains.

_____   3. At least one of the trains that had been involved in the crash ran on diesel fuel.

_____   4. Rescuers thought of and rejected several ideas for saving Vitek before they decided on trying the method that finally worked.

_____   5. If it had been summer, digging the hole would have taken a longer time.

Score 5 points for each correct answer.

_____   **Total Score:** Making Inferences

D   Using Words Precisely

Each numbered sentence below contains an underlined word or phrase from the article. Following the sentence are three definitions. One definition is closest to the meaning of the underlined word. One definition is opposite or nearly opposite. Label those two definitions using the following key. Do not label the remaining definition.

C—Closest   O—Opposite or Nearly Opposite

1. Michalski's job was to <u>monitor</u> train traffic *inside* the yard.

    _____   a. set into motion

    _____   b. oversee

    _____   c. pay no attention to

2. He had to hold his breath whenever he dropped his face into the <u>rancid</u> pool of diesel fuel.

    _____   a. sticky

    _____   b. rotten and foul-smelling

    _____   c. fresh and sweet-smelling

3. They even managed to lift the pile a little bit—but not nearly enough to <u>extricate</u> Vitek, who had fallen into a slight depression in the ground.

    _____   a. pull out

    _____   b. push back

    _____   c. identify

4. It was <u>tedious</u> work and progress was slow....

    _____   a. exciting

    _____   b. tiresome and dull

    _____   c. important

5. ...after three hours of <u>painstaking</u> drilling the rescuers had chiseled an opening wide enough for Vitek's body.

_____ a. casual

_____ b. painful

_____ c. extremely careful and thorough

_____ Score 3 points for each correct C answer.

_____ Score 2 points for each correct O answer.

_____ **Total Score:** Using Words Precisely

Enter the four total scores in the spaces below, and add them together to find your Reading Comprehension Score. Then record your score on the graph on page 197.

Score	Question Type	Lesson 20
_____	Finding the Main Idea	
_____	Recalling Facts	
_____	Making Inferences	
_____	Using Words Precisely	
_____	**Reading Comprehension Score**	

Author's Approach

Put an X in the box next to the correct answer.

1. The author uses the first sentence of the article to
   - ☐ a. capture the reader's interest.
   - ☐ b. describe what it is like to work in a rail yard.
   - ☐ c. compare train travel and travel by air.

2. What is the author's purpose in writing "Near Death in a Rail Yard"?
   - ☐ a. To encourage the reader to travel only by car
   - ☐ b. To inform the reader about a resourceful group of rescuers
   - ☐ c. To describe a situation in which someone was almost killed on purpose

3. Choose the statement below that is the weakest argument for using an air-powered chisel for rescuing Rich Vitek.
   - ☐ a. The air-powered chisel was safe.
   - ☐ b. The air-powered chisel was available.
   - ☐ c. The air-powered chisel was slow.

4. How is the author's purpose for writing the article expressed in paragraph 17?
   - ☐ a. The paragraph suggests that Don Eddy enjoyed talking about the rescue after it was over.
   - ☐ b. The paragraph mentions that Vitek suffered nerve damage and spinal disk problems.
   - ☐ c. The paragraph points out that Vitek is still alive only because of the efforts of his rescuers.

_____ Number of correct answers

Record your personal assessment of your work on the Critical Thinking Chart on page 198.

Summarizing and Paraphrasing

Follow the directions provided for question 1. Put an X in the box next to the correct answer for question 2.

1. Look for the important ideas and events in paragraphs 15 and 16. Summarize those paragraphs in one or two sentences.

_____

_____

_____

2. Below are summaries of the article. Choose the summary that says all the most important things about the article but in the fewest words.

☐ a. Rich Vitek should consider himself a very lucky man. After all, he was buried under a 20-foot-high pile of debris. Rescuers worked feverishly trying to save him. Even though he suffered injuries, he is now alive.

☐ b. A train with no brakes was wrongly routed into a busy rail yard where it ran into another engine. Rich Vitek was trapped underneath a pile of debris created by the crash. Rescuers dug a hole next to the debris, using an air-powered chisel, and were able to slide Vitek out. Even though he suffered injuries, Vitek survived.

☐ c. Rescuers, including firefighter Don Eddy, thought through their plan thoroughly before deciding to use the air-powered chisel to save Rich Vitek. They worked for about three hours, taking 20-minute turns drilling into the frozen ground before they rescued Vitek.

_____ Number of correct answers

Record your personal assessment of your work on the Critical Thinking Chart on page 198.

Critical Thinking

Follow the directions provided for questions 1 and 3. Put an X in the box next to the correct answer for the other questions.

1. For each statement below, write O if it expresses an opinion or write F if it expresses a fact.

_____ a. The Burlington Northern train left the Northtown rail yard at 11:15 P.M. on February 14, 1996.

_____ b. Eddy kept Vitek informed of the efforts that the rescuers were making.

_____ c. Train brakes should be constructed better so that this kind of accident is impossible.

2. Judging by the events in the article, you can predict that the following will happen next:

☐ a. laws will be passed to stop freight trains from traveling so fast.

☐ b. the train's engineer will be fired.

☐ c. officials will try to find out why the switch was set improperly.

3. Read paragraph 6. Then choose from the letters below to correctly complete the following statement. Write the letters on the lines.

According to paragraph 6, _____ because _____.

a. the runaway train crashed into another engine

b. a switch had been set improperly

c. workers were going about their business at 11:15 P.M.

4. What did you have to do to answer question 3?

☐ a. find an opinion (what someone thinks about something)

☐ b. find a comparison (how things are the same)

☐ c. find a cause (why something happened)

_____ Number of correct answers

Record your personal assessment of your work on the Critical Thinking Chart on page 198.

Personal Response

What was most surprising or interesting to you about this article?

_____

_____

_____

_____

Self-Assessment

One good question about this article that was not asked would be

_____

_____

_____

_____

and the answer is

_____

_____

_____

_____

CRITICAL THINKING

FLIGHT TO FREEDOM

Orestes Lorenzo is surrounded by his family—(from left) wife Victoria and sons Alejandro (6) and Reyniel (11)—after his daring rescue of them from Cuba.

t's a suicide mission," a friend warned Orestes Lorenzo. One small mistake and Cuban rockets would blow Lorenzo and his plane out of the sky.

2   But Lorenzo, a former Cuban Air Force major, had already made up his mind: he would try to rescue his wife Vicky and their two young sons, Reyniel and Alejandro. As he put it, "I would rather die than leave my family [in Cuba]."

3   Orestes Lorenzo hadn't always felt that way. Born in Cuba and raised under the communist dictatorship of Fidel Castro, Lorenzo had grown up thinking of himself as a loyal communist. He even became a war hero as a combat jet pilot in Angola. Later, however, he went to Moscow to study. He was there when new freedoms were bringing an end to communism in Russia. Lorenzo liked what he saw and began to have second thoughts about communism. When he returned home to Cuba, he bristled under the cruel rule of Castro. "How can I tolerate it when my children can't think the way they want?" he asked Vicky.

4   In March of 1991, Lorenzo decided to bolt Cuba and head for the United States.

Tens of thousands of Cubans had done the same thing before him. Most of these refugees left by boat. But Lorenzo took a different approach: he climbed into the cockpit of his jet fighter plane and headed north for Florida. Eighteen minutes later he landed at the Key West naval air station and asked for political asylum. One of the men who greeted him smiled and said, "Welcome to the United States."

5   Lorenzo had, however, made one huge miscalculation. He expected Castro would let his wife and children join him. Lorenzo felt sure "the Cuban government would be so embarrassed by my defection that they would allow my family to leave." Besides, Vicky and the children had visas to enter the United States. But as the family soon discovered, Castro wasn't about to cooperate. "Your husband had the guts to fly off in a [jet] to America," one Cuban official taunted Vicky. "Now let's see if he has the guts to come back and get you."

6   Refusing to give up hope, Vicky clung to the belief that her husband would come back for her and the boys. "If you are not able to leave," Lorenzo had said to her before he left, "I will be back for you. I may come in a balloon, a plane, a boat, or swimming. But I'll be back."

7   Vicky tried to be patient, but it wasn't easy. Cuban officials began to harass her, telling her lies about her husband. They said he was a traitor to Cuba and that he was going to marry another woman. Vicky never believed a word of it.

8   Meanwhile, after many months of appeals, it was clear to Lorenzo that Castro would never change his mind. Determined to reunite his family, Lorenzo recalled the words of his six-year-old son, Alejandro. During a rare phone call, the boy had begged his father to come and get them. "Daddy, you are a pilot. Come get us in a helicopter. Fly over the house and drop down a ladder."

9   Well, of course, it wouldn't be that easy, Lorenzo knew, but perhaps some sort of air rescue was possible. Lorenzo met with a human rights group that promised to help him. Elena Amos, a member of the group, gave him $30,000 to buy an old Cessna plane that could hold six people. Slowly, a plan for his "suicide mission" began to take shape. Yes, he would fly to Cuba and get his family.

The Cessna airplane that Orestes Lorenzo used to land on a Cuban beach to rescue his wife and sons

10   If he was caught, he knew he would most likely be shot, but it was a risk he was desperate enough to take.

11   Using third-party contacts, Lorenzo smuggled coded messages to Vicky. The deception and timing had to be perfect. Vicky and the boys would go to Mamey Beach on the north coast of Cuba, pretending to be on a seaside picnic. They were to dress in fluorescent orange hats and shirts so they would be easy to spot. In one coded message, Lorenzo told Vicky to "please send the children shoes in sizes 5½ and 6½." He was trying to communicate that the pickup would be between 5:30 P.M. and 6:30 P.M.

12   On December 19, 1992, everything was ready. At 5:05 P.M. Lorenzo took off from a small landing strip in Florida. On his lap, he cradled a map of the Cuban coast. For his plan to work, he had to fly just 10 feet above the waves. That was the only way to avoid being spotted by Cuban radar.

13   At 5:00, Vicky and the boys walked to the rendezvous site. At exactly 5:43, Vicky saw a plane flying low over the water; she knew it was Lorenzo preparing to land. "Run, run!" she cried to the boys. "It's Daddy!"

14   As Lorenzo looked out his window, however, he saw trouble. There, in the middle of the coastal road that he intended to use as a runway, sat a large boulder. A tall road sign was also in his path. Worst of all, on this normally deserted stretch of road, a bus was attempting to pass a truck.

15   This was no time to sweat the small stuff, however. Lorenzo had to land; he didn't have a moment to waste. At any second, Cuban authorities might show up and destroy his chances of success. Using his skill as a highly-trained pilot, he tilted his wings and cleared the boulder and the road sign by inches. The truck and bus were still headed straight for him, but both drivers managed to swerve and avoid him. Lorenzo landed hard on the road, slammed on his brakes, and popped a quick U-turn. One wing of the plane barely missed the truck. Lorenzo later said he would never forget the stunned look on the truck driver's face.

16   Quickly, Vicky and the kids jumped into the plane. It had been 20 long months since they had seen Lorenzo; they wanted to celebrate with hugs and kisses. But there was no time for that. Lorenzo hustled them into their seats as fast as possible, knowing that if they didn't get away fast, they might still be shot down by a Cuban missile.

17   With his family safely on board, Orestes Lorenzo took off and headed north to Florida and freedom. Only after he reached American air space, 22 minutes later, did he feel safe. Then he raised his hand and shouted, "I did it! There's your answer, Castro! I did have the guts." After that, he turned and welcomed the hugs and kisses of Vicky, Reyniel, and Alejandro. 🍃

If you have been timed while reading this article, enter your reading time below. Then turn to the Words-per-Minute Table on page 195 and look up your reading speed (words per minute). Enter your reading speed on the graph on page 196.

Reading Time: **Lesson 21**

_____ : _____
Minutes   *Seconds*

Finding the Main Idea

One statement below expresses the main idea of the article. One statement is too general, or too broad. The other statement explains only part of the article; it is too narrow. Label the statements using the following key:

M—Main Idea **B—Too Broad** **N—Too Narrow**

_____ 1. Cruel governments sometimes drive their citizens to acts of desperation.

_____ 2. After Orestes Lorenzo defected to the United States, he assumed that the Cuban government would allow his wife and sons to join him, but he was mistaken.

_____ 3. In a daring daytime rescue, former Cuban jet pilot Orestes Lorenzo flew his wife and children out of Cuba and headed for freedom in the United States.

_____ Score 15 points for a correct M answer.

_____ Score 5 points for each correct B or N answer.

_____ **Total Score:** Finding the Main Idea

B **Recalling Facts**

How well do you remember the facts in the article? Put an X in the box next to the answer that correctly completes each statement about the article.

1. Lorenzo had served the Cuban government as a jet fighter in
☐ a. South Africa.
☐ b. Spain.
☐ c. Angola.

2. Lorenzo made his own escape from Cuba by
☐ a. boat.
☐ b. jet fighter plane.
☐ c. train.

3. Lorenzo received the $30,000 to buy an old plane from
☐ a. a member of a human rights group.
☐ b. the U.S. government.
☐ c. his family in Cuba.

4. To rescue his family, Lorenzo landed on a stretch of road near
☐ a. Havana, Cuba.
☐ b. Mamey Beach, Cuba.
☐ c. Miami Beach, Florida.

5. Upon landing, Lorenzo had to avoid a
☐ a. large boulder in the middle of the road.
☐ b. police car.
☐ c. telephone pole.

Score 5 points for each correct answer.

_____ **Total Score:** Recalling Facts

C | Making Inferences

When you combine your own experience and information from a text to draw a conclusion that is not directly stated in that text, you are making an inference. Below are five statements that may or may not be inferences based on information in the article. Label the statements using the following key:

C—Correct Inference   **F—Faulty Inference**

_____   1. Orestes Lorenzo proved his courage in many situations.

_____   2. To Lorenzo, safety was more important than freedom.

_____   3. Key West, Florida, is located just a short distance from Cuba.

_____   4. Elena Amos was a fairly wealthy woman.

_____   5. It was not at all important to Castro that Cuban citizens remain in Cuba.

Score 5 points for each correct answer.

_____ **Total Score:** Making Inferences

D | Using Words Precisely

Each numbered sentence below contains an underlined word or phrase from the article. Following the sentence are three definitions. One definition is closest to the meaning of the underlined word. One definition is opposite or nearly opposite. Label those two definitions using the following key. Do not label the remaining definition.

C—Closest   **O—Opposite or Nearly Opposite**

1. When he returned home to Cuba, he <u>bristled</u> under the cruel rule of Castro.

    _____   a. became upset and angry

    _____   b. lived

    _____   c. calmed down

2. Eighteen minutes later he landed at the Key West naval air station and asked for political <u>asylum</u>.

    _____   a. exposure to harm

    _____   b. safety and protection

    _____   c. opinions

3. Lorenzo felt sure "the Cuban government would be so embarrassed by my <u>defection</u> that they would allow my family to leave."

    _____   a. behavior

    _____   b. agreement or approval

    _____   c. abandonment

4. "Your husband had the guts to fly off in a [jet] to America," one Cuban official <u>taunted</u> Vicky.

    _____   a. spoke with respect

    _____   b. mocked

    _____   c. explained to

5. Cuban officials began to <u>harass</u> her, telling her lies about her husband.

_____ a. follow

_____ b. annoy over and over

_____ c. please

_____ Score 3 points for each correct C answer.

_____ Score 2 points for each correct O answer.

_____ **Total Score:** Using Words Precisely

Enter the four total scores in the spaces below, and add them together to find your Reading Comprehension Score. Then record your score on the graph on page 197.

Score	Question Type	Lesson 21
_____	Finding the Main Idea	
_____	Recalling Facts	
_____	Making Inferences	
_____	Using Words Precisely	
_____	**Reading Comprehension Score**	

Author's Approach

Put an X in the box next to the correct answer.

1. What does the author mean by the statement "In March of 1991, Lorenzo decided to bolt Cuba and head for the United States"?

☐ a. Lorenzo decided to escape Cuba and go to live in the United States.

☐ b. Lorenzo decided to leave Cuba temporarily and visit the United States.

☐ c. Lorenzo wanted to punish Cuba by becoming a United States citizen.

2. From the statements below, choose those that you believe the author would agree with.

☐ a. Orestes Lorenzo was not the type of person who gives in easily.

☐ b. The Cuban government was being unreasonable when it wouldn't allow Lorenzo's family to join him.

☐ c. Elena Amos of the human rights group should not have risked so much money on a possible suicide mission.

3. The author probably wrote this article in order to

☐ a. express an opinion about the Cuban government.

☐ b. inform the reader of a daring rescue.

☐ c. create a mood of tension in the reader.

4. The author tells this story mainly by

☐ a. telling about events in the order they happened.

☐ b. comparing different topics.

☐ c. telling different stories about the same topic.

_____ Number of correct answers

Record your personal assessment of your work on the Critical Thinking Chart on page 198.

Summarizing and Paraphrasing

Follow the directions provided for questions 1 and 2. Put an X in the box next to the correct answer for question 3.

1. Complete the following one-sentence summary of the article using the lettered phrases from the phrase bank below. Write the letters on the lines.

> **Phrase Bank:**
> a. Lorenzo's rescue of his family
> b. Lorenzo's escape
> c. Orestes Lorenzo's early years

After a short introduction, the article about "Flight to Freedom" begins with_____, goes on to explain_____, and ends with_____.

2. Reread paragraph 5 in the article. Below, write a summary of the paragraph in no more than 25 words.

_____

_____

_____

Reread your summary and decide whether it covers the important ideas in the paragraph. Next, decide how to shorten the summary to 15 words or less without leaving out any essential information. Write this summary below.

_____

_____

3. Choose the best one-sentence paraphrase for the following sentence from the article:

"Refusing to give up hope, Vicky clung to the belief that her husband would come back for her and her boys."

☐ a. Vicky had unshakable faith that her husband would return for his family.

☐ b. Vicky never stopped hoping that her husband would return to the United States.

☐ c. Vicky clung to her boys while she hoped that her husband would rescue her.

> _____ Number of correct answers
>
> Record your personal assessment of your work on the Critical Thinking Chart on page 198.

Critical Thinking

Follow the directions provided for questions 1, 2, and 5. Put an X in the box next to the correct answer for the other questions.

1. For each statement below, write O if it expresses an opinion or write F if it expresses a fact.

_____ a. Elena Amos gave Lorenzo $30,000 to buy an old Cessna plane.

_____ b. If he had really loved his family, Lorenzo would never have left them alone in Cuba.

_____ c. The rescue plan called for Vicky and the boys to meet Lorenzo at a beach on Cuba's north coast.

2. Choose from the letters below to correctly complete the following statement. Write the letters on the lines.

In the article, _____ and _____ are different.

a. Lorenzo's opinion about communism while serving as a combat jet pilot

b. Lorenzo's opinion about communism while growing up

c. Lorenzo's opinion about communism after returning from Moscow

3. What was the cause of Lorenzo's dismay when he saw the road he intended to land on?

☐ a. The road was nearly blocked by a boulder and a tall road sign.

☐ b. The road was filled with Cuban soldiers.

☐ c. He couldn't see his wife or sons where he expected them to be.

4. Of the following theme categories, which would this story fit into?

☐ a. Old friends are the best friends.

☐ b. Might makes right.

☐ c. Where there's a will, there's a way.

5. In which paragraph did you find your information or details to answer question 3?

_____

_____ Number of correct answers

Record your personal assessment of your work on the Critical Thinking Chart on page 198.

Personal Response

This article is different from other articles about rescues I've read because

_____

_____

_____

_____

and Orestes Lorenzo is unlike other rescuers because

_____

_____

_____

_____

Self-Assessment

Before reading this article, I already knew

_____

_____

_____

_____

Compare and Contrast

Think about the articles you have read in Unit Three. Choose the four rescues that took the most *creative* thought and planning. Write the titles of the articles that tell about them in the first column of the chart below. Use information you learned from the articles to fill in the empty boxes of the chart.

Title	Was the rescue accomplished by a group or by one person acting alone?	How much time did the rescuers have to make their plans?	Which part of the rescue showed creative thinking?

Write a message to one group of rescuers explaining why you admire them. _____

_____

_____

Words-per-Minute Table

Unit Three

Directions: If you were timed while reading an article, refer to the Reading Time you recorded in the box at the end of the article. Use this words-per-minute table to determine your reading speed for that article. Then plot your reading speed on the graph on page 196.

Lesson No. of Words	15 1116	16 917	17 939	18 1223	19 978	20 1134	21 1115	
1:30	744	611	625	815	652	756	743	**90**
1:40	670	550	563	734	587	680	669	**100**
1:50	609	500	512	667	533	619	608	**110**
2:00	558	459	470	612	489	567	558	**120**
2:10	515	423	433	564	451	523	515	**130**
2:20	478	393	402	524	419	486	478	**140**
2:30	446	367	376	489	391	454	446	**150**
2:40	419	344	352	459	367	425	418	**160**
2:50	394	324	331	432	345	400	394	**170**
3:00	372	306	313	408	326	378	372	**180**
3:10	352	290	297	386	309	358	352	**190**
3:20	335	275	282	367	293	340	335	**200**
3:30	319	262	268	349	279	324	319	**210**
3:40	304	250	256	334	267	309	304	**220**
3:50	291	239	245	319	255	296	291	**230**
4:00	279	229	235	306	245	284	279	**240**
4:10	268	220	225	294	235	272	268	**250**
4:20	258	212	217	282	226	262	257	**260**
4:30	248	204	209	272	217	252	248	**270**
4:40	239	197	201	262	210	243	239	**280**
4:50	231	190	194	253	202	235	231	**290**
5:00	223	183	188	245	196	227	223	**300**
5:10	216	177	182	237	189	219	216	**310**
5:20	209	172	176	229	183	213	209	**320**
5:30	203	167	171	222	178	206	203	**330**
5:40	197	162	166	216	173	200	197	**340**
5:50	191	157	161	210	168	194	191	**350**
6:00	186	153	156	204	163	189	186	**360**
6:10	181	149	152	198	159	184	181	**370**
6:20	176	145	148	193	154	179	176	**380**
6:30	172	141	144	188	150	174	172	**390**
6:40	167	138	141	183	147	170	167	**400**
6:50	163	134	137	179	143	166	163	**410**
7:00	159	131	134	175	140	162	159	**420**
7:10	156	128	131	171	136	158	156	**430**
7:20	152	125	128	167	133	155	152	**440**
7:30	149	122	125	163	130	151	149	**450**
7:40	146	120	122	160	128	148	145	**460**
7:50	142	117	120	156	125	145	142	**470**
8:00	140	115	117	153	122	142	139	**480**

Minutes and Seconds

Seconds

Plotting Your Progress: Reading Speed

Unit Three

Directions: If you were timed while reading an article, write your words-per-minute rate for that in the box under the number of the lesson. Then plot your reading speed on the graph by putting a small X on the line directly above the number of the lesson, across from the number of words per minute you read. As you mark your speed for each lesson, graph your progress by drawing a line to connect the X's.

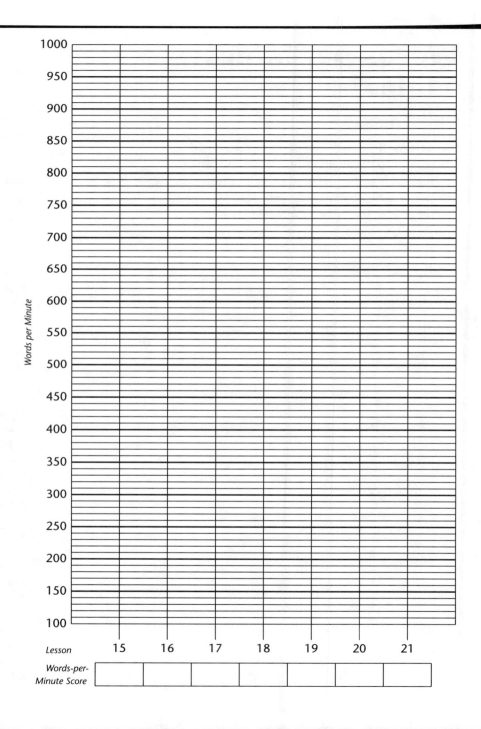

Words per Minute

Lesson	15	16	17	18	19	20	21
Words-per-Minute Score							

Plotting Your Progress: Reading Comprehension

Unit Three

Directions: Write your Reading Comprehension score for each lesson in the box under the number of the lesson. Then plot your score on the graph by putting a small X on the line directly above the number of the lesson and across from the score you earned. As you mark your score for each lesson, graph your progress by drawing a line to connect the X's.

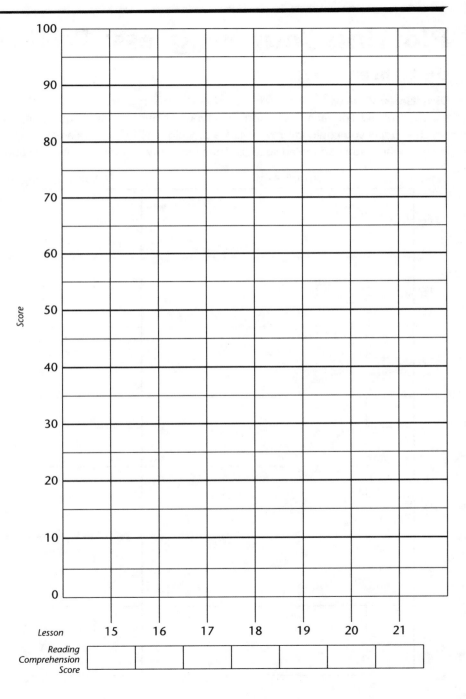

Plotting Your Progress: Critical Thinking

Unit Three

Directions: Work with your teacher to evaluate your responses to the Critical Thinking questions for each lesson. Then fill in the appropriate spaces in the chart below. For each lesson and each type of Critical Thinking question, do the following: Mark a minus sign (–) in the box to indicate areas in which you feel you could improve. Mark a plus sign (+) to indicate areas in which you feel you did well. Mark a minus-slash-plus sign (–/+) to indicate areas in which you had mixed success. Then write any comments you have about your performance, including ideas for improvement.

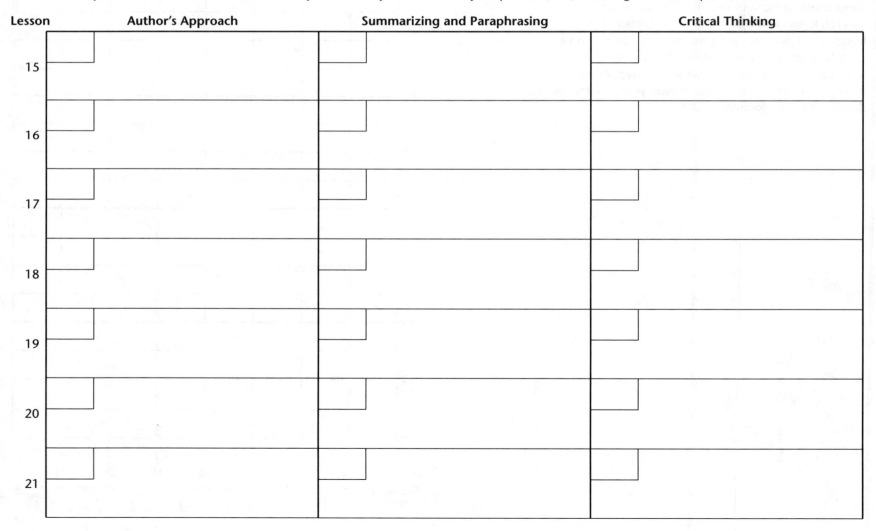

Lesson	Author's Approach	Summarizing and Paraphrasing	Critical Thinking
15			
16			
17			
18			
19			
20			
21			

Photo Credits